Animals in Heaven?

Animals in Heaven?

A Catholic Pastoral Response
to Questions about Animals

TERRY MARTIN

Foreword by Andrew Linzey

WIPF & STOCK · Eugene, Oregon

ANIMALS IN HEAVEN?
A Catholic Pastoral Response to Questions about Animals

Copyright © 2024 Terry Martin. All rights reserved. Except for brief quotations in critical publications or reviews, no part of this book may be reproduced in any manner without prior written permission from the publisher. Write: Permissions, Wipf and Stock Publishers, 199 W. 8th Ave., Suite 3, Eugene, OR 97401.

Wipf & Stock
An Imprint of Wipf and Stock Publishers
199 W. 8th Ave., Suite 3
Eugene, OR 97401

www.wipfandstock.com

PAPERBACK ISBN: 979-8-3852-2675-7
HARDCOVER ISBN: 979-8-3852-2676-4
EBOOK ISBN: 979-8-3852-2677-1

VERSION NUMBER 080724

Laudato Si', On Care for our Common Home, Encyclical Letter of Pope Francis © Dicastero per la Comunicazione-Libreria Editrice Vaticana. Used with permission.

Scripture quotations are from the ESV® Bible (The Holy Bible, English Standard Version®), © 2001 by Crossway, a publishing ministry of Good News Publishers. Used by permission. All rights reserved.

*In memory of my grandparents Clarice and Ronald Ellis:
ever unconditionally loving.*

While Francis was journeying near the city of Siena, he came on a great flock of sheep in the pastures. When he had given them gracious greeting, as was his wont, they left their feeding, and all ran toward him, raising their heads, and gazing fixedly on him with their eyes. So eagerly did they acclaim him, that both the shepherds and the Brethren marvelled, beholding around him the lambs, and the rams no less, thus wondrously filled with delight.

At another time, at Saint Mary of the Little Portion, a lamb was brought unto the man of God, which he thankfully received, by reason of the love of guilelessness and simplicity that the lamb's nature doth exhibit. The holy man exhorted the lamb that it should be instant in the divine praises and avoid any occasion of offence unto the Brethren; the lamb, on its part, as though it had observed the piety of the man of God, diligently obeyed his instructions. For when it heard the Brethren chanting in the choir, it too would enter the church, and, unbidden of any, would bend the knee, bleating before the altar of the Virgin Mother of the Lamb, as though it were fain to greet her. Furthermore, at the election of the most holy Body of Christ in the solemn Mass, it would bend its knees and bow, even as though the sheep, in its reverence, would reprove the irreverence of the undevout, and would incite Christ's devout people to revere the Sacrament.

THE LIFE OF ST. FRANCIS OF ASSISI BY ST. BONAVENTURE[1]

---

1. Bonaventure, *Life of St. Francis*, ch. 8, §7.

Contents

Foreword by Andrew Linzey | ix
Acknowledgements | xi
Abbreviations | xiii
Introduction | xv

1. Why Did God Create Animals? | 1
2. How Does the Catholic Church View Animals? | 13
3. What about the Ethical Treatment of Animals and the Idea of Animal Rights from a Catholic Perspective? | 23
4. Are There Animals in Heaven? | 30
5. Can Animals Teach Us Anything about Our Faith and about Our Belief in God? | 39
6. Does the Resurrection of Jesus Make a Difference for Animals? | 46
7. What about Animals and the Holy Mass? | 56
8. How Does the Holy Spirit Help Us to Understand Animals? | 68
9. What Can the Catechism Tell Us about Animals? | 76
10. Is It Appropriate to Pray for Animals and to Bless Them? | 85
11. Why Does God Allow Animals to Suffer? | 94
12. Why Did St. Francis Preach to the Birds? | 101
13. What about the Popes? | 109
14. Why Are There So Many Stories and Legends Associated with Saints? | 120
15. Is an Authentic View of Animals Continuing to Develop and Grow within the Church? | 126

Conclusion: An Animal Friendly Church? | 136

Bibliography | 141

Foreword

Andrew Linzey

FATHER TERRY IS DOING a new thing. Over the past two decades, there has been a marked increase of theological work relating to animals, mostly by academics. But such work has almost entirely overlooked one important aspect. It is this: the pastoral dimension.

Christian faith needs theology of course. But it is only one dimension of the church's life. Christians need to be fed by many dimensions, and, most notably, for almost all people this has to include pastoral contact with a priest, who can encourage, inspire, and help parishioners to develop their personal journey in faith. Not least, it requires thoughtful attention to the pressing questions that parishioners ask about the current state of the world, including our responsibility for creation and especially about the status of animals. The papal encyclical *Laudato Si'* has clearly put these concerns on the Catholic agenda.

The special value of this book is the way in which it frankly addresses and explores the basic questions that many animal-regarding Christians ask about animals: Will they meet their companion animals again in heaven? Do animals have souls? Do animals have rights? What precisely does the church teach?

Fr. Terry responds to these questions (and more) utilising the riches of the Catholic tradition. He emphasises the often-overlooked importance of the spiritual bond between humans and animals. And he invites people to enlarge their spiritual feeling for fellow creatures.

The result is a remarkable book: a terrific read, full of humour, personal anecdotes, and disarming self-deprecation—all drawing on the best in Christian thought. Its pastoral nature is pioneering and powerful. Altogether, a warming and inspiring read. It deserves a wide readership.

Foreword

The Reverend Professor Andrew Linzey is the director of the Oxford Centre for Animal Ethics and has been a member of the Faculty of Theology in the University of Oxford for twenty-eight years. He has written or edited more than forty books, including *Animal Theology* (University of Illinois Press, 1994), *Why Animal Suffering Matters: Philosophy, Theology, and Practical Ethics* (2009), and *Animal Theologians* (2023), both published by Oxford University Press.

Acknowledgements

I AM GRATEFUL TO my bishop, the Right Reverend Richard Moth, Bishop of Arundel and Brighton, and to the priests and deacons of the diocese, for indulging me with a twelve-month sabbatical and thus allowing this small project to come to fruition. Fr. David Osborne has kindly ministered to the lovely people of the parish of Worthing and Lancing in my absence. To him too, I offer thanks.

Thanks must also go to my parishioners, family, and friends for their ceaseless patience, support, and curiosity. One or two priest-colleagues, in particular, have buoyed me up when that was needed, and kept my feet firmly on the ground where appropriate. Mostly, and they know who they are, they have gently, and with wisdom, allowed me the freedom to raise ideas for discussion and to reflect, with them, on the matters and issues which this book attempts to raise.

I first encountered the Reverend Professor Dr. Andrew Linzey at a Summer School in Oxford in 2023. We had previously communicated by email, but I hadn't had the pleasure of meeting him in person. Without Andrew, this book simply would not have happened. He said to me, at that gathering in Oxford, "Do it for the animals." That specific endorsement of this project has given me the energy and the confidence to get to this stage. Andrew's wisdom, expertise in the field (having had so many works published himself), and general encouragement (with constructive criticism) has helped to make this book what it is. I thank him, additionally, for kindly providing the foreword for this volume. I will always owe him a huge debt of gratitude.

Equally, I am immensely grateful to Dr. Deborah M. Jones who, with kindness and skill, generously read through the whole manuscript and offered comments and reflections. Her help and advice has hugely enhanced this project.

Acknowledgements

I also need to say thank you to those who raised difficult questions concerning the book, or who challenged my assumptions and conclusions. They have assisted in making my research and my writing all the more thorough.

Finally, I offer thanks to the team at Wipf and Stock for their unfailing courtesy and diligence.

Abbreviations

CBCEW: Catholic Bishops' Conference of England and Wales
CCC: *Catechism of the Catholic Church*
CCCC: *Compendium of the Catechism of the Catholic Church*
LD: *Laudate Deum*, apostolic exhortation of Pope Francis
LS: *Laudato Si', On Care for our Common Home*, encyclical of Pope Francis

Introduction

The wild beasts will honour me, the jackals and the ostriches,
for I give water in the wilderness, rivers in the desert,
to give drink to my chosen people.
The people whom I formed for myself, that they might declare my praise.
(ISAIAH 43:20)

ONE ORDINARY SUNDAY MORNING, at the end of Mass, I was standing at the door of the church, greeting parishioners as they left. I could see Maureen discreetly hovering in the porch, and I quickly guessed that she probably wanted a "quick word." These pastoral conversations are very valuable and it's important to give them time, not least because Sunday Mass may actually be the only opportunity a parishioner has to speak to their priest.

"Father," said Maureen, "will Izzy go to heaven?" Izzy is a beautiful tortoise-shell cat who was rescued from a life of cruelty and neglect, but who is now a fantastic companion to Maureen. I had met Izzy a few times and enjoyed interacting with her when visiting Maureen at her home for a coffee. Would Izzy go to heaven? It was an important question, and in the moment, I did my best to come up with something of an answer. However, I wanted to know more. Where does the Catholic Church stand on the question of animals and heaven? Do animals have souls? What is God doing when he creates animals—and why? This book is an ordinary parish priest's attempt to consider some of these issues. Whilst it is inevitably, to some degree, a work of theology (in the sense that all questions about God must be), it is, first and foremost, a pastoral response, a priest-to-parishioner conversation around these important matters. As we shall see, the church has not always provided a specific answer to many of these questions, but I hope that my long years of ministry have given me some opportunities to consider such concerns, albeit from a pastoral perspective (since that is my lived experience).

There are some brilliant, easily available books which systematically cover this whole area much better than I can: incisive works which cut to the heart of the matter and look at all of the important theological, spiritual, ethical, and biblical issues. Here, I attempt to open up a discussion with Maureen (and with all people of good will) on how we can make sense of our everyday experience of faith, and to look at the questions which parishioners frequently, and with good reason, raise. Thus, this book is a response to all who ask the big questions about God and animals. I have tried to offer reasonable, balanced, carefully considered pastoral answers to difficult questions, answers which are drawn from the church's experience of what God the Father is like, who Jesus is, the role of the Holy Spirit, and how we, as Catholics and as Christians, interact with the whole world: creation, humans, animals, and plants.

I provide opportunities to delve into *Laudato Si'*, the encyclical letter of Pope Francis of 2015, calling us to take care of our common home, planet earth. Additionally, at the end of each chapter, there are possibilities for brief moments of prayer; always rooting this endeavour in the heart of the church and in a legitimate spirit of intercession.

Some years ago, despite firm protestations from friends and family, I went ahead and gave a home to two dogs. It is entirely true to say that these lovely creatures (Pepe and Georgie) changed my life. They became (and remain) my constant companions, often making me laugh, and always offering me unconditional affection and love. In many ways, it is this up-close-and-personal relationship with these charming dogs that has brought me to the point of writing down these pastoral considerations.

Ultimately, this book is a fruit of both my reflections on faith and, within that perspective, of my relationship with all of God's animals (not just dogs). It is offered as an opportunity for people of faith to think with me about how we relate to animals and who, under God, animals are. This is also a space for me to praise God for the beauty and diversity of creation, and to invite fellow Catholics, other Christians, and all people, to consider our relationship with God concerning animals. This is not an exhaustive consideration of the issues at hand. No pastoral reflection can be. Drawing on the Scriptures, the saints, the church fathers, the popes, a few poets, and with some reference to contemporary theologians, I offer the following

Introduction

for discussion and reflection. You may come away, in fact, with as many questions as answers; so be it. If I can stimulate and provoke serious consideration of the issues I raise, my task will be complete.

I'm doing this for the animals because I care about them; because they matter to me; because my faith in Jesus Christ means that I must. St. Bonaventure said, "God is the origin, exemplar, and end of every creature.... Every creature is by its nature a kind of effigy and likeness of the eternal Wisdom. Therefore, open your eyes, alert the ears of your spirit, open your lips and apply your heart, so that in all creatures you may see, hear, praise, love and worship, glorify and honour your God."[2] Amen to that!

I refer often to "animals" and "humans" in this work. For clarity's sake, I accept, of course, that humans are animals, but I have chosen (with one or two exceptions) not to repeatedly speak of, for example, "human and non-human animals," but simply to employ common usage, as generally understood.

Throughout, all biblical quotations are taken from the English Standard Version—Catholic Edition (ESV—CE).

terry.martin@abdiocese.org.uk

---

2. Bonaventure, *Soul's Journey*, cited in Linzey and Regan, *Compassion*, 9.

1

Why Did God Create Animals?

Are not five sparrows sold for two pennies?
And not one of them is forgotten before God.

(LUKE 12:6)

THE BIBLE IS FULL of animals. They appear on page after page, and even Jesus himself takes time to include them in his preaching and teaching. Over 120 different species are mentioned: from majestic lions (Amos 3:8; Rev 5:5) to humble sparrows (Luke 12:6), sheep (Ps 23; John 10:11), lambs (Exod 12:3–13; Rev 5:6), snakes (Gen 3:1 and 10:16), calves (Exod 32; Luke 15:23), and so many more. All these creatures dot the narrative and pages of the Holy Scriptures, the divinely inspired word of God. Jesus refers to them in, for example, Matt 23:37 when he reflects on how he would have gathered the people of Jerusalem "together as a hen gathers her brood under her wings," and the same Gospel writer tells us that John the Baptist sees the Spirit of God descending on Jesus "like a dove" (Matt 3:16).

Christians believe, of course, especially from their reading of the book of Genesis in the Bible, that God freely chose to create animals when he formed the heavens and the earth, the sea and the dry land, the fruit and the trees, and human beings too. On the fifth and sixth days of creation, just before he created the beginnings of the human race, God created animals, whom he blessed and whom he declared were good (Gen 1:20–25). Having created the animals, each in their varying kinds, God tells them to go forth and multiply; to share, as it were, by the process of creation and recreation, in that developing organic action with which God himself is engaged. What a blessing: to participate in the very life of God in this way. Of course, all elements of creation are willed, freely chosen, gratuitous acts of the creator. God creates, God forms anew, God reforms, and God renews the different elements of his creation perfectly. Taking the Scriptures at face value, we can see that animals, from the moment of their creation, share and participate in some elements of the very nature of God.

The *Catechism of the Catholic Church* supports this wonderful vision of creation as being a participator and sharer in God's own creative nature: "By the very nature of creation, material being is endowed with its own stability, truth and excellence, its own order and laws. Each of the various creatures, willed in its own being, reflects in its own way a ray of God's infinite wisdom and goodness. Man must therefore respect the particular goodness of every creature, to avoid any disordered use of things which would be in contempt of the Creator and would bring disastrous consequences for human beings and their environment."[1]

In the earliest chapters of the book of Genesis, many scholars refer to a "peaceable kingdom" (a term originally derived from Isa 11:1, as translated in the old King James Version of the Bible). The peaceable kingdom, which God creates out of love and for love, is where plants, animals, and human beings all exist in perfect harmony. In this, the entirety of creation as we know it, there is a mutual sense of every individual part of God's created order knowing its own position within the whole, and respecting the proper place, in God's plan, of each of the other parts. More than that, the first couple of chapters give us a beautiful vision of what we can presume God intends for the world: "And God said, 'Behold, I have given you every plant yielding seed that is on the face of the earth, and every tree with seed in its fruit. You shall have them for food. And to every beast of the earth and to every bird of the heavens and to everything that creeps on the earth, everything that has the breath of life, I have given every green plant for food.' And it was so. And God saw everything that he had made, and behold, it was very good" (Gen 1:29–31).

The prophet Isaiah, prophesying within the context of the coming of the long-awaited Messiah, has a wonderful vision of a kingdom where peace and harmony reign. Such a kingdom will see the end of weeping and crying;

---

1. *CCC*, §339.

health and strength will exist for young and old alike; there will be houses in which to dwell and vineyards rich with fruit; and, most importantly, this kingdom will see an end to violence and cruelty, promoting security and compassion for all: "They shall not hurt or destroy in all my holy mountain for the earth shall be full of the knowledge of the Lord as the waters cover the sea" (Isa 11:9). In this kingdom a remarkable generosity and mutuality will exist, and all creatures will respect and honour one another, rejoicing in their complementary difference and living together in peace as one. What a wonderful world God has given to us and what hope there is in seeking and living the friendship and love of such a kingdom. Further, Isaiah's dramatic vision is of the kingdom which will be established by the Christ who, when he returns, will liberate and bring to wholeness all created things. Jesus will inaugurate anew, as it were, a perfect Garden of Eden, restoring the original peaceable kingdom in all its magnificent fullness.

It is interesting to note that the food which God provides for his people in this kingdom is abundant and does not require the taking of life from any living being: "I have given you every plant yielding seed that is on the face of all the earth, and every tree with seed in its fruit. You shall have them for food" (Gen 1:29). As humans and animals coexist in harmonious peace, there is no violence or suffering, even for dietary purposes. The diet of plants and trees is bountiful and given for nurture and for nourishment. The crown of God's creation is, of course, man and woman, who are uniquely and beautifully created in the image and likeness of God's own self (Gen 1:27), and God has provided food in copious amounts for their need. God's self-giving love is never-ending but, for now, his work is done and he rests. On the day that he takes pause, the seventh day, God declares that particular day holy, blessing it, having stated that his creation is "very good" (Gen 1:31). The heaven for which we are made is now created on earth, and God can rest, since his creation is very good. The perfect holiness of the sabbath consists in rest, and in the eating of the plants and the fruit which the humans have been given by God himself.

In these passages, there is a real sense of perfection, union, and compassion—a perfection, union, and compassion which will be seen again and concretely manifested, in due course, in Jesus Christ.

I get a tiny glimpse of this original peaceable kingdom from my two dogs, Pepe and Georgie, who always and everywhere bring me so much joy. I completely understand that for many of us with companion animals there is a sense of family, of finding mutual happiness and peace together, and of celebrating our difference. Because I'm not a dog, I can't think like a dog, but I can instinctively tell when my dogs are happy, sad, excited, or afraid. This is no human projection, where I cast my own feelings onto my canine companions but, rather, a very evident and real expression of what they feel. Georgie will often look at me and make a little barking noise if he thinks it's time to go out for a walk; he seems very talented at reading the clock. Actually, I am convinced that both he and Pepe can tell the time!

Sometimes, I find myself preaching at Mass about the dogs who, for me, are wonderful homily resources. I feel that I have learned from them so much about life. My own life is incomparably different from how it was before they came along. I am happier, more settled, and content to just be with them. Curiously, I would say that they, in their particular manner, are one of the important ways in which the face of God is revealed to me; they have helped me to grow in faith and to deepen my relationship with God. It is hard to imagine that they are anything other than part of God's gift to me, as a way of fostering my own flourishing in faith.

It is important to note too, of course, that there are, alongside Pepe and Georgie, many other aspects of my life which promote and deepen a sense of faith: I draw immense inspiration, for example, from so many selfless, dedicated men and women in the parishes in which I've ministered; the Mass always touches me profoundly and renews my heart; prayer provides a constant source of peace and joy; music strikes and energises me; the Sussex Downs leave me breathless with wonder. There is so much that God offers as a way of showing me his closeness to creation. My dogs, and by extension, all animals are, for me, part of that benevolent divine revelation.

So, why *did* God create animals? Perhaps God made animals to showcase and reveal the beauty of his created order. We cannot fail to see the immense wonder and power of the orca diving through the waves, or the beauty of the peacock strutting his stuff, or the contentment of the mother cow with her calf. It's as if God had a field-day in showing, through animals, his power and beauty and inventiveness (always remembering, of course, that human beings are the supreme example of this, for we are animals too). That's to say nothing of all those creatures that dwell in the depths of the sea or in the highest heavens, about whom we know so little and who, in their own particular ways, speak to us of the grandeur of God. Think of the platypus, or the axolotl, or the pangolin. Go look them up, if those names are new to you; you will be amazed. Each of them seems to tell us yet more about the extraordinary God who made them and in whom they find life and sustenance.

The more that we explore the reality of who God is, the more we find ourselves uncovering the amazing creatures with which we, as human beings, share this planet. It's as if it's all a part of his plan. Pope Benedict speaks movingly in one of his books[2] and in his Encyclical Letter, *Caritas in Veritate* (2009), where he reminds readers and hearers that there exists a "covenant between human beings and the environment, which should mirror the creative love of God, from whom we come and towards whom we are journeying."[3] The catechism again reminds us of this truth: "God created the world to show forth and communicate his glory. That his creatures should share in his truth, goodness and beauty—this is the glory for which God created them."[4]

If, drawing on the biblical evidence, men and women are those who have dominion (Gen 1:26) over this wonderful and extraordinary world, as Catholics and other Christians believe, then we have a huge responsibility indeed. These creatures, as varied and diverse as it's possible to conceive, are a reminder to us of our God-given duty to protect and nurture the planet and all that exists within. The earth is God's, surely. The animals are God's, surely. We are God's too; but, uniquely, we human beings have an obligation (burden, even) to care for and to till (to serve) the earth. "The Lord God took the man and put him in the Garden of Eden to work it and keep it" (Gen 2:15). Humanity is called to be a keeper of the planet and its inhabitants; we are to laboriously shape it and to allow it, with God's good help, to grow and to flourish. This is, essentially, a relationship of service, not of control or domination. What a beautiful vocation: to serve the world and, in so doing, to cooperate with God in bringing this planet to full fruition, sustaining the whole of creation with all the peace and harmony with which God invests it, and which is part of his self-giving revelation and love. We *must* be servants of the planet! This is an essential call from God to the man in the garden; to do otherwise means that the man (and, with him, all of humanity) will "surely die" (Gen 1:17). Death is clearly not part of God's original plan for his creation. The world and all created beings are not playthings over which men and women have inexhaustible power and control. The whole of creation, including all creatures who inhabit the

2. Benedict XVI, *Garden*, §50, 69.
3. Benedict XVI, *Caritas in Veritate*, §7.
4. *CCC*, §319.

planet, is entrusted to human beings, not to be exploited, but to be cared for and looked after, for the mutual benefit of all.

Perhaps animals are essential for the well-being of the planet—not just to show us the greatness of God, but to help us all to coexist and to grow through the balance of nature. We are constantly reminded, for example, of the importance of bees in the ecosystem. We might not generally give too much time in our everyday lives to thinking about bees and other such remarkable insects as butterflies and hoverflies. But these creatures are surely a part of God's plan to nurture and sustain the planet, and they do not happen to exist accidentally. In fact, bees are vital to the earth in supporting healthy and secure food systems and supplies, and in ensuring that we have the nutritious and colourful foods that we have for so long enjoyed. Their particular skill is pollination and, when they execute this brilliant talent, it is a beautiful sight to behold. The essential role of pollinator that bees have, enables the plants which they visit to grow, multiply, and to produce our food. Bees allow and create, in their tiny buzzy-buzzy ways, a veritable harvest of good things for us to enjoy. Add to this the vast numbers of wildflowers that rely on bees for their production and growth and we can see how precious these insects are and how that, without them, we cannot really continue to exist in the ways to which we have become so accustomed. There are something like twenty thousand different species of bee across the globe and, of the around two hundred and seventy species that exist in the UK alone, the more familiar honeybee is just one of this vast multitude.

What a vast array of wonders for us to enjoy . . .

Returning to the book of Genesis, we could say that God creates humans and animals as companions for one another. Primarily, God creates animals for his own glory, as seen above—or rather, the very existence of all created beings, is a sign of the glory which we properly direct to God. Yet, the peaceable kingdom is a place where there is a certain cordiality, and where no species (at least at first) is dependent on another. All coexist harmoniously and in peace, as we have noted. In Gen 2:18–20, before creating the woman, God creates animals as possible companions to the man, and brings them to the man for him to name them. In this, the man exercises his authority as being created in the image and likeness of God, since only God has the authority to "name." We could strongly argue that it is as a result of his desire for humans to have friends that God appears to bring the animals to the man. God's desire is that the man should not be alone, but that he will flourish when he has companionship and friendship. I'm sure that we can all relate to that. Ultimately, of course, it is in the creation of the woman that the man discovers his authentic partner and soul friend. Together, the man and the woman exist joyously at first with the animals—animal kind and humankind celebrating both their difference and their complementarity. With the playing out of this particular narrative, we can see that animals have inherent value in and of themselves, that in being named they are specifically set apart, and that they are, in fact, *more* than just companions for human beings.

Perhaps you've seen the film *Hachi*?[5] Drawing on an original story from 1987,[6] it tells the true story of a Japanese Akita dog who was beyond loyal to his human friend. Having been rescued by Hidesaburō Ueno and given a home, Hachi forever attached himself to his human guardian, travelling with him to the railway station each morning to see him off to work and then, as if by clockwork, dashing back at the appropriate time to meet him returning home from the train. Hachi was always there; he never missed, and always so joyfully greeted Hidesaburō on his return. That is until, sadly, one day Hidesaburō failed to come back. Hachi waited and waited, but to no avail. Sadly, Hachi's human companion had suddenly died while at work and would never be coming home again. In an act of immense love and devotion, Hachi continued every day, for the rest of his own life, at the correct time, to rush to the station to seek out and meet his homecoming friend. This he did for nine whole years, until his death in 1935. If you go to Shibuya Railway Station in Tokyo, to this day you can see the statue of Hachi, erected by both the family of Hidesaburō Ueno, and by the grief-stricken station staff, who had also come to know and love the Akita dog. Hachi continues, in Japan, to be used often as an example of faithfulness and loyalty. You know, perhaps, the more familiar story of Greyfriars Bobby, a Skye terrier who guarded his human companion's grave for fourteen years until his own death, and whose monument I was happy, recently, to visit in Edinburgh.

In 2015, Pope Francis published his groundbreaking encyclical on the importance of caring for creation. *Laudato Si', On Care for our Common Home* invites the whole of humanity to consider various environmental and ethical issues and, as part of this reflection, draws some attention to animals. Reflecting on the words of Ps 148, where we read that "[God]

---

5. *Hachi: A Dog's Tale*, directed by Lasse Hallström, 2009.
6. *Hachikō Monogatari*, directed by Seijirō Kōyama, 1987.

commanded and they were created. And he established them for ever and ever; he gave a decree, and it shall not pass away" (5b–6), the Holy Father urges us to notice and respect the laws of nature and the delicate balance that exists between all the creatures of the world: "The laws found in the Bible dwell on relationships, not only among (human) individuals but also with all other living beings."[7] He goes on, in the same paragraph to mention a couple of examples from the Scriptures where this view is endorsed. *Laudato Si'* emphasises the importance of respecting and caring for all creatures on the earth (not just the human ones). The overriding thrust of the encyclical is that animals are, of course, part of God's creation and have intrinsic value in and of themselves, and not in relation to what they can be or do for humankind: "By their mere existence they bless him and give him glory"[8] and "may the Lord rejoice in his works" (Ps 104:31).

We remember that in the book of Genesis there are two creation narratives as found in chapter 1 and chapter 2. Those narratives, along with other biblical references to creation, such as, for example, Ps 104 and the latter part of the book of Job, really attempt to do the impossible and to tell us how the world came into being. Whether we see these accounts as factual or allegorical, they are how we, as Catholics, understand the creation of the world.

Christian theologians, through the ages, have attempted to make greater sense of the creation stories which we see in the Bible and have concluded various theories about why/how God created the world: some say that God creates because he can't help himself—that creation is a dynamic expression of his love, a love that is not static but energetic and which is compelled to go out from the depths of his heart. We might all recognise that genuine love cannot contain itself, and that it needs to find some sort of tangible expression. So, God's love is seen in a fruitful and material way in his free creation of the world. God cannot resist but to pour forth his love. We could happily agree that authentic love is always creative, always focussed on the other, and always fruitful.

It is very much within this context that we can choose to situate the creation of animals, and the beginnings of a reflection as to why they exist. Part of God's fruitful creativity (which, of course, is an aspect of his loving nature) means that animals and human beings share a certain status: that of having been created by God. In that sense, there is a degree of

---

7. Francis, *LS*, §68.
8. *CCC*, §2416.

understandable sameness (even though we are so different) that is shared by animals and humans: each existing and deserving to exist because each is created lovingly by God. Neither seems to be a random accident, from a Christian understanding, but a willed and purposeful creation by a loving creator. The highly regarded St. Gregory of Nyssa (ca. 335–ca. 394), a great defender of Christian orthodoxy and theology, powerfully proclaims the presence of God in every aspect of his creation: "For when he considers the universe, can anyone be so simple-minded as not to believe that the Divine is present in everything, pervading, embracing and penetrating it? For all things depend upon Him who is, and nothing can exist which does not have its being in Him who is."[9]

The writers of the book of Genesis do not attempt to tell us *why* God creates humans and animals and plants and seas—just that he does. We, as faithful believers, seek to make sense of that creation and to understand God's plan for the world through this lens.

My maternal grandfather used to take me to Mass on Sundays. He was a quiet, thoughtful man who was liked and respected by all who knew him. He has been dead for some years now, but there is a distinctive feature about him that very much stays with me. When he prayed aloud during the liturgy, he did so with great definition. It seemed to me then and now, that he genuinely desired to mean what he was saying. Two examples of this are particularly vivid: the Our Father (which many of us are perhaps tempted say rather quickly with a lifetime's absent-minded familiarity), and the Creed. When he said the Creed, I truly believe that he meant every word. Each time I lead the people in the saying of the Nicene Creed at Mass, even today, I think of him.

During Mass this morning I was pondering, in some of the more still moments, on the issues that this chapter raises. However, rather than letting my mind wander here and there, I tried to echo the qualities of my grandfather, cherishing each word, and desiring to speak it with deliberation and care. Then something struck me. We understand and confidently proclaim that God made heaven and earth, but let's not forget that he also made, as we confidently say in the Creed, *all* things "visible and invisible."[10] God cannot be limited, as it were, to our human experience of the earth, or to our partial understanding of the world's existence. On the contrary, God's inventiveness and power in creating the world is to be celebrated and

---

9. Hardy and Richardson, *Later Fathers*, cited in Linzey and Regan, *Compassion*, 8.
10. See Nicene Creed in the *Roman Missal*, 562.

cherished. We can see and touch *some* animals; we know that they exist. But there's so much about them that we have still to learn; there is an "invisibility" to our knowledge around who animals are and what the love of God has in store for them. We can certainly and confidently say that God creates animals for his own glory, and not for you and not for me. It is in their own being that animals praise the creator.

God creates the animals for himself, and to move them (and us) to the natural worship of a loving creator. It seems perfectly acceptable to take this stance and to see how easily it sits with our Catholic understanding of the universe. Visible or invisible, from the majestic hugeness of the blue whale (up to one hundred feet long and weighing-in at a massive two hundred tons), to the infinitesimally small demodex follicorum (just 0.3 millimetres long), it seems that God knows what he is doing when he creates these animals and that we are more than blessed to share the planet with them.

Maybe we would want to say, too, that God creates the animal kingdom because we human beings can potentially learn so much from these creatures. The fact that animals have no recognisable voice (in human terms) and so often come under the care and the stewardship of humans, means that we are invited to treat them with compassion and kindness and understanding; indeed, they very often need us to be their advocates. This seems to me to be a natural response for the follower of Jesus. Christians, like others, can often be heard loudly to declare their love for animals; that's understandable enough. God seems to have planted within us, for the most part, a natural sense of realising that the animals we see around us are intended to be a part of who we are, since they, like us, are a part of his dream for creation; they can, for example, teach us about love and life. Their very existence can constantly challenge us to be compassionate towards these creaturely neighbours with whom we find ourselves sharing the planet.

Sometimes, unsurprisingly, we allow ourselves the freedom of giving moral purpose to animals. Think about the stories of Hachi or Greyfriars Bobby, where we talk of the dog as being "loyal" and "faithful." There is no doubt that a great deal about the animal kingdom teaches us so much of what it means to be human. There are hard lessons there also, of course, and much about the natural ways of the animal kingdom can challenge us—but maybe that's good for us too: we do not, for example, need to be predators in order to live. The fact that some animals necessarily live in this way (like lions and many other free-roaming animals) prompts us to recall the immense freedom that God has given particularly to humans, as a sign of our dignity and status. We can make choices that many of the animals cannot make for themselves, and that may remind us of our immense responsibility and duty to make compassionate and charitable choices for them and for us—because we can. What an amazing thought: that God would give animals to us to help us to become better human beings. When we know our need of God, we are in the right place, and maybe animals help us to see that need. Perhaps animals can assist us in that quest to live as God would want us to live. "Know that the Lord, he is God! It is he who made us, and we are his; we are his people, and the sheep of his pasture" (Ps 100:3).

Mother Julian of Norwich (born 1342) puts it better than I can when she speaks beautifully of the manner in which God beholds even the smallest part of his creation: "And he showed me a little thing, the size of a hazelnut, on the palm of my hand, round like a ball. I looked at it thoughtfully and wondered, 'What is this?' And the answer came, 'It is all that is made.' I marvelled that it continued to exist and did not suddenly disintegrate; it was so small. And again my mind supplied the answer, 'It exists, both now and for ever, because God loves it.' In short, everything owes its existence to the love of God. In this little thing I saw three properties. The first that God made it. The second that God loves it. The third that God keeps it."[11]

From Laudato Si', Pope Francis

> "By the word of the Lord, the heavens were made" (*Ps 33:6*). This tells us that the world came about as the result of a decision, not from chaos or chance, and this exalts it all the more. The creating word expresses a free choice. The universe did not emerge as the result of arbitrary omnipotence, a show of force or a desire for self-assertion. Creation is of the order of love. God's love is the fundamental moving force in all created things: "For you love all things that exist and detest none of the things that you have made; for you would not have made anything if you had hated it" (*Wisdom 11:24*). Every creature is thus the object of the Father's tenderness, who gives it its place in the world. Even the fleeting life of the least of beings is the object of his love and, in its few seconds of existence, God enfolds it with his affection. St Basil the Great described the Creator as "goodness without measure" (*Hexaemeron*) while Dante Alighieri spoke of the "love which moves the sun and the stars" (*The Divine Comedy*). Consequently, we can

---

11. Julian of Norwich, *Revelations*, 10.

ascend from created things "to the greatness of God and to his loving mercy" (Benedict XVI, *Catechesis* 2005).[12]

Prayer

O God, enlarge within us the sense of fellowship with all living things. We pray for our brothers and sisters, the inarticulate beasts, to whom you gave the earth as their home in common with us. We remember with shame that in the past we have exercised the high dominion of humanity with ruthless cruelty so that the voice of the earth, which should have gone up to you in song, has become a groan of anguish and a cry of torment. May we realise that these creatures live not for us alone, but for themselves and for you, and that they too love all the sweetness of life. Through Jesus Christ our Lord. Amen. *(Attributed to St. Basil the Great)*[13]

---

12. Francis, *LS*, §77.
13. Catholic Concern for Animals, "Prayers," § 12.

2

How Does the Catholic Church View Animals?

*Ask the beasts and they will teach you;
the birds of the heavens, and they will tell you.*

(JOB 12:7)

THROUGHOUT THE GENERATIONS, THE saints have had a very special relationship with animals. The history of the church is littered with examples of animals and holy men and women learning from one another, praising God together, and revealing Christian virtues one to the other. Many of the saints simply couldn't contemplate cruelty to animals, for example, and saw, in these creatures of nature, the reality of the presence of God. We will return to these thoughts later.

St. Bede writes affectionately of his near contemporary, St. Cuthbert of Lindisfarne. St. Cuthbert lived in the seventh century and was renowned for his holiness, for his sympathetic understanding of animals, and for his instinctive awareness of animals as created by God. A popular story relates how it became clear to those around him, that Cuthbert was habitually disappearing from the monastery at nighttime and then, having slipped quietly away, returning in the morning. Arousing curiosity from the brothers, a fellow monk was sent to spy on Cuthbert, and to find out what was going on, cautiously following him from a distance. As he watched, he saw

Cuthbert wade into the sea, right up to his neck, and stay there throughout the night in a spirit of prayer, penance, and contemplation. As morning came, the saint left the water, knelt on the beach, and prayed further. Extraordinarily, as Bede notes, while he prayed, "two otters bounded out of the water, stretched themselves out before him, warmed his feet with their breath, and tried to dry him with their fur. They finished, received his blessing, and slipped back to their watery home."[1]

There's more. Cuthbert, as well as being the patron saint of otters, is often associated with crows and ravens. In the latter part of his life, feeling the need for more time to pray, and having a desire for greater solitude, he took himself away to Inner Farne, a small and bleak island in the North Sea, off the coast of Northumberland. On one occasion, a small flock of ravens decided that they'd rather like the straw on the roof of Cuthbert's house for their nests, so they began to help themselves. Cuthbert was not amused and rebuked them. But they took no notice. Resorting to firmer language, and drawing on his strong faith, Cuthbert retorted, "In the name of Jesus Christ, depart forthwith." At this, the ravens left. St. Bede continues the story: "Three days later, one of a pair of them returned, and finding Cuthbert digging, stood before him, with feathers outspread and heads bowed low to their feet as if in a sign of grief. Using whatever signs they could to express contrition, they very humbly asked pardon. When Cuthbert realised what it meant, he gave permission for them all to return. Back they came with a fitting gift, which Cuthbert would often show proudly to his visitors."[2]

These lovely stories (and there are so many similar tales of saints and their interaction with animals) do not tell us why God created animals, but they do affirm that humans and animals have been created to live in peace and to coexist harmoniously, sometimes very obviously to the mutual advantage of each. There are also contemporary accounts of men and women who have, for whatever reason, found themselves interacting with crows, ravens, or other corvids, and who describe the natural and endearing habit of these birds to bring gifts. St. Bede's description of St. Cuthbert, in the light of contemporary experience, has an authentic ring of truth to it. The early Christian author Tertullian (160–240), a real apologist for the truths of the gospel, wrote that "cattle and wild beasts pray, and bend their knees, and in coming forth from their stalls and lairs look up to heaven, their mouths not idle, making the spirit move in their fashion. Moreover,

---

1. Bede, *Age of Bede*, 54.
2. Bede, *Age of Bede*, 71.

the birds taking flight lift themselves up to heaven and, instead of hands, spread out the cross of their wings, while saying something which may be supposed to be a prayer."[3]

Following his Baptism in the river Jordan, Jesus (as recorded in Mark 1:12) is "driven" out into the wilderness by the Spirit, there, for forty days and forty nights, to prepare for his ministry. The poet Robert Graves (1895–1985) meditates on this experience of Jesus being with the wild animals, pondering his ministry and his destiny:

> Then ever with him went,
> Of all his wanderings
> Comrade, with ragged coat,
> Gaunt ribs—poor innocent—
> Bleeding foot, burning throat,
> The guileless young scapegoat:
> For forty nights and days
> Followed in Jesus' ways,
> Sure guard behind him kept,
> Tears like a lover wept.[4]

In the Scripture passage, we are told that, during this time, "[Jesus] was with the wild animals, and the angels ministered to him" (Mark 1:13). These brief verses from St. Mark are fascinating. Throughout his gospel, the evangelist presents the stories and sayings of Jesus in a distinctly vivid and compact way. He chooses his words carefully. St. Mark clearly feels that the time of Jesus in the wilderness "with the wild animals" is a significant feature of that whole experience. The implication is, of course, from the text, that Jesus coexisted peacefully and harmoniously with those creatures. St. Mark does not say that Jesus was afraid of the animals, or that he had to kill and eat them, or that there was a concern for Jesus around the presence or meaning of the animals. No, very noticeably, the peace of the scene as depicted by St. Mark is such that the angels can readily come and minster to Jesus. It is a picture of kinship and tranquillity and unity. Jesus and the animals—at such a crucial time in the life of Jesus—are one. We could go even further and say that it is *after* the experience of the temptations that the animals associate with Jesus, almost as if they are part of a joyful divine celebration of his fortitude. Although the story of the temptation of Jesus also appears in the gospels of Matthew and Luke (Matt 4:1–11; Luke

3. Tertullian, *On Prayer*, cited in Linzey and Regan, *Compassion*, 7.
4. Graves, "In the Wilderness."

4:1–13), it is Mark alone who characteristically includes this dramatic little detail and draws particular attention to the presence of the animals.

St. Thomas Aquinas (1224–1274) is often known as the Angelic Doctor. He is considered by many to be perhaps the greatest theologian that the church has ever known. This thirteenth-century Dominican friar sought to make sense of all the questions that are raised by belief in God. His greatest and most famous work is the *Summa Theologiae*, in which he literally attempts to sum up, in a definitive way, all matters concerning philosophy and theology. Animals are not without mention in his writings. The Greek philosopher Aristotle (384–322 BC), an influence on Aquinas, had already declared that animals are inferior to humans because, whereas humans can apply the use of reason, animals cannot. Aristotle suggested that, therefore, men and women may freely use animals without the due and necessary consideration which they could be expected to show to one another. Drawing on both Aristotle and on St. Augustine of Hippo (AD 354–430), who also appears to have been sympathetic to Aristotle's views,[5] Aquinas raises the question of how and why animals exist.

Generally, St. Thomas speaks of animals only in relation to humans and this is an important aspect of his work. In a nutshell, this brilliant theologian concluded that animals were not a proper object of moral concern because God has made them for human use (to ride, to wear, to labour, to eat, and so on) and particularly because they (in contrast to human beings) cannot think rationally.[6] Aquinas has hugely influenced the church's view of animals for over eight hundred years. For a Catholic, to challenge or to question the commonly received orthodoxy of St. Thomas, who is such an outstanding, revered, and eminent scholar, can feel like a betrayal of all that one holds sacred. Since the time of this teaching, the church has seemingly accepted as definitive the views and teachings of St. Thomas Aquinas, and the important conversations around this issue, at least at first glance, can appear to have stopped there.

The issue was more clearly outlined with contributions from the French Catholic philosopher, René Descartes (1596–1650), writing some 350 years later. Descartes declared that animals were "material automata" (robots, really) because they lack language and general intelligence and, most significantly he says, because they cannot feel pain.[7] He suggested that

---

5. Augustine, *City of God*, 1.20.
6. Aquinas, *Summa Contra Gentiles*, 112.
7. Descartes, *Discourse*, 50.

even though animals are living, organic creatures, they are, ultimately, just like machines. Scholars further recall that the philosopher liked to practise the science of vivisection on animals, and that when the animals cried out in the throes of agony, he quickly and dismissively likened the response to the sound of a machine that was functioning improperly. A crying dog, Descartes maintained, is no different from a whining gear that needs oil.[8] St. Thomas Aquinas doesn't go this far, but Descartes is very clear in saying that, because they cannot experience pain, animals are therefore undeserving of human compassion. Only human beings, he states, matter in this way. (As an aside to this idea, we could be forgiven for thinking that not much has changed since the time of Descartes. Today, throughout the world, large numbers of dogs, mice, monkeys, and guinea pigs, among others, are cruelly confined in laboratories in order to be used in painful and invasive scientific experiments, from which they suffer greatly.)

A brief summary of this view may conclude that, ultimately, animals don't matter either to humans or to God. Influential theologians have, with these and similar views, apparently stifled any further discussion on the matter. We can all, perhaps, see the inner conflict that arguments like these raise up. We want to accept and digest the teachings of the church, for we know that they are life-enhancing, and yet our lived experience is that animals *do* have feelings, that they can express joy and fear and excitement and aggression and much more besides. Those familiar with domesticated animals like dogs and cats will know how cheeky and clever their companion animal can be. A visit to an animal sanctuary will reveal similar traits in sheep and pigs and cows and chickens. We've all seen amazing wildlife documentaries too, where the ingenuity of free-roaming animals to hide and to escape danger, and to warn others of impending attack and so on, is admirable. It is self-evident to us today that animals are not mere machines and that they draw from us so much more than that which makes them useful to us. It seems to me that it's acceptable, in a spirit of charity, to challenge the orthodoxy of the church's tradition in this context and to realise that, like the Scriptures, this teaching is understandably rooted in a historic time and place and that the truths which it reveals need to be seen through the lens of where we are, as a church, today. Timeless truths remain timeless only if appropriately interpreted and received for all times, surely?

As an ordinary parish priest, I would be cautious in saying that the teachings of St. Thomas Aquinas (especially) and René Descartes are open

8. Francione, *Introduction*, xxii.

to question, but I would say that we, as those who have informed our consciences through the teaching of the church, are free to relate that teaching to today's experience and to say that, organically, our understanding of the world, of animals, of the whole of creation, has adapted and grown in a way that is noticeably different to that as seen in the lived experience of Aquinas or Descartes. We would not easily say that we know better than these great teachers, but that maybe we have come to understand somewhat differently, partly because the teachings that we have received have shaped and formed us into thinking this way. Pope Francis, in paragraph 92 of *Laudato Si'*, appears to effectively overturn Aquinas where he says, "Every act of cruelty towards any creature, is contrary to human dignity." Aquinas, the great thirteenth-century Dominican teacher, challenged by Francis, the twenty-first century Jesuit pope? Unthinkable.

St. Philip Neri (1515–1595) is known best as the founder of the Oratory, a religious congregation within the church. What is not so well known is his choice to be a vegetarian for reasons of animal welfare, and for his conscious decision to avoid, where he could, causing suffering to animals. Well-known throughout the city of Rome for his beloved cat companion, with whom he happily shared his monastic cell, St. Philip would frequently set captive birds free and, when given gifts such as live partridge for food, would prefer to release them and delight in their freedom as he watched them fly away. He even urged kindness to flies and other insects, seeing them too as created by God and deserving of compassion and care. On passing a butcher's shop he famously stated that "if everyone was like me, they wouldn't kill animals."[9] Neri was not deterred from revealing, by his words and actions, that animals do matter, that they are not insignificant machines who feel nothing and whose lives are of no consequence.

I have seen, first hand, the influence that companion animals can have over their human guardians. Animals very often bring out the best in us. I remember visiting Joan, an elderly parishioner, who had enjoyed a long and happy life but who now, after the death of her beloved husband, was feeling alone and afraid. Her caring family, concerned and anxious for her, decided to present her with a cheeky and playful kitten. What a difference Missy made to Joan's life. Missy brought laughter and joy back to Joan's daily experience in a way that could not have been envisaged. The beginnings of her depression and withdrawal were lessened and were helped hugely by Missy's bold and attractive good nature. I also saw a side to Joan

---

9. "Saints Who Loved Animals," §9.

that I'd never seen before; a tenderness and a warmth, especially when she was talking about Missy. She once told me that Missy had saved her life! I completely believe her. We know, I'm sure, of similar stories among our own family and friends.

The current teaching of the Catholic Church around animals can be found in four short paragraphs of the *Catechism of the Catholic Church*.[10] The catechism reveals a somewhat ambiguous tone in its view of animals, and it is possible to draw varied conclusions from the text. We learn, for example, that "human dominion over inanimate and other living beings granted by the creator is not absolute; . . . it requires a religious respect for the integrity of creation."[11] Earlier, we looked briefly at the idea of dominion and of God's call to humans to care for our earthly home and for all beings within. The following paragraph of the catechism, much beloved of animal advocates, is clear: "Animals are God's creatures. He surrounds them with his providential care. By their mere existence they bless him and give him glory. Thus, humans owe them kindness. We should recall the gentleness with which saints like St Francis of Assisi or St Philip Neri treated animals."[12]

Animals naturally look to God as their creator and equally naturally praise him for being such. They help us, as human beings, to raise our own hearts and voices to the divine. In paragraph 2417, the catechism uses the word "stewardship" as a kind of synonym for "dominion." This is a helpful idea and implies a role for humanity more given to care, to compassion, and to service, than to the more hierarchical sense that "dominion" could be seen to imply "God entrusted animals to the stewardship of those whom he created in his own image."[13] This section goes on to suggest that it is "legitimate" to use animals for food and clothing and to "domesticate" animals for human use in things like work and leisure. Even medical experiments are permitted "within reasonable limits." Unfortunately, those reasonable limits are not clearly spelled out and the catechism fails to look at the usefulness, or otherwise, of such experiments.[14]

Finally, with a clarity which is to be welcomed, the catechism states that "it is *contrary to human dignity* to cause animals to suffer or die needlessly,"[15]

---

10. *CCC*, §2415–18.
11. *CCC*, §2415.
12. *CCC*, §2416.
13. *CCC*, §2417.
14. *CCC*, §2417.
15. *CCC*, §2418; my emphasis.

a statement echoed by Pope Francis himself in *Laudato Si'*, as quoted above. Whilst I commend these four paragraphs, I suggest that it may be possible to be left with as many questions as answers by the catechism (at which we will look more closely later). Suffice to say that the teaching of the church, certainly from Aquinas onwards, needs to be viewed, first and foremost, alongside the overarching principle of love and compassion to all, as observed in the peaceable kingdom of Genesis. This love and compassion is, of course, perfectly exemplified in the life of Jesus, and seen in his words and actions from the gospels. We remember, too, that love is, primarily, an ethical choice (not merely a whimsical feeling)—a choice which we can decide to make again and again. "God is love, and whoever abides in love abides in God, and God abides in him" (1 John 4:16).

Karl Barth (1886–1968), a renowned theologian and teacher, provides some helpful insight for us. His view of animals, and of their place in creation, seems to me to be entirely consistent with an authentic Catholic worldview. "[The] world of animals and plants forms the indispensable living background to the living-space divinely allotted to man and placed under his control. As they (the animals) live, so can he. He is not set up as lord over the earth, but as lord on the earth which is already furnished with these creatures. Animals and plants do not belong to him; they and the whole earth belong only to God. . . . [God] expects a conscious and deliberate recognition of His honour, mercy and power."[16] It may seem strange to mention a major Protestant theologian here (even though Pope Pius XII is believed to have declared him the greatest theologian since St. Thomas Aquinas; a claim it seems impossible to verify), but Barth's contribution in shaping Christian thinking and theology in modern times cannot be overstated.

St. Thomas More (1478–1535), so revered among Catholics in the British Isles was, as well as being Lord High Chancellor of England, a holy and faithful servant of the church. Ultimately, he would die a martyr's death for his convictions in the Catholic faith. His famous work *Utopia* (1516) expresses his desire for a political state where brutality and cruelty are reduced as much as possible. As such, he was repulsed by those who perpetuate violence of any sort, and he extends this view to include violence towards animals. Despite being a perfect English gentleman, he rejected hunting, even though it was a hugely popular pursuit of the wealthy and powerful of his time. In his vision of a perfect political state, he asserts that those who

16. Barth, *Dogmatics*, vol. III/4, 350.

kill and butcher animals can never be seen as properly belonging to society and suggests that in (his perfectly imagined) Utopia there will be no such absence of kindness and compassion: "The Utopians feel that slaughtering our fellow creatures gradually destroys the sense of compassion, which is the finest sentiment of which our human nature is capable. . . . If the hope of slaughter and the expectation of tearing in pieces the beast doth please thee, thou shouldst rather be moved with pity to see a silly innocent hare murdered by a dog: the weak of the stronger, the fearful of the fierce, the innocent of the cruel and unmerciful. Therefore all this exercise of hunting, as a thing unworthy to be used of free men, the Utopians have rejected to their butchers. . . . For they count hunting the lowest, the vilest and most abject part of butchery, . . . whereas the hunter seeketh nothing but pleasure of the silly and woeful beast's slaughter and murder."[17] It is unlikely that St. Thomas More was a vegetarian but, clearly, if he is reluctant to accept the slaughter and butchery of animals (indeed, in his view, the Utopians would never do such a thing), it is only those who, in his terms, are beneath such a perfect society (he speaks of "slaves") that are worthy of forgiveness for such an act.

Despite his words seeming polemical to us, I suggest that More's vision is exactly where we find ourselves today. Billions of factory-farmed animals are killed annually for human consumption, often in the most grim and detestable of conditions; yet most of us are spared having to consider what goes on behind those high abattoir walls. Others do the work of slaughtering and butchering for us (usually those who have extremely limited options for employment, such as poorly paid immigrants). Slaughterhouses are hidden in plain sight and safeguarded like fortresses, so that what takes place in them may not disturb those who choose to eat the products of their industry. St. Thomas More was no mere plaster-cast saint, but a man engaged with the world who spoke out clearly for animals. As a faithful Catholic, his desire to see generosity accorded to all creatures readily flows from his aspiration to be like Christ, for whom compassion and love are central.

---

17. More, *Utopia*, 73.

From Laudato Si', Pope Francis

> It is enough to recognise that our body itself establishes us in a direct relationship with the environment and with other living beings. The acceptance of our bodies as God's gift is vital for welcoming and accepting the entire world as a gift from the Father, and our common home, whereas thinking that we enjoy absolute power over our own bodies turns, often subtly, into thinking that we enjoy absolute power over creation.[18]

Prayer to St. Francis

Good St. Francis, you loved all of God's creatures. To you, the animals in all their rich diversity were your brothers and sisters. Help us to follow your example of treating every living being with kindness and with compassion. St. Francis, patron of animals, pray for us and for the creatures which God has given to us; show us the way to praise God with and in his creation, as you so faithfully did. Amen. St. Francis, pray for us!

(Traditional)[19]

---

18. Francis, *LS*, §155.
19. "Blessing of the Animals," §24.

3

What about the Ethical Treatment of Animals and the Idea of Animal Rights from a Catholic Perspective?

*It is I who by my great power and my outstretched arm
have made the earth,
with the men and animals that are on the earth,
and I give it to whomever it seems right to me.*

(JEREMIAH 27:5)

I WAS ONE OF over two thousand priests concelebrating at the huge outdoor Mass, with an overall attendance of something like half a million people. Pope Benedict XVI, having arrived by helicopter the evening before, was presiding at the Mass. The sun shone, the music was joyful, and a vast number of faithful Catholics were sharing in the experience. The year was 2008 and we were in Sydney, Australia, for World Youth Day. It was quite an experience.

As part of the whole World Youth Day package, our group had been billeted with some local Australian families. I found myself staying on an enormous farm just outside Sydney, with a family who lived more outdoors than in. They were warm, welcoming, and nothing was too much trouble. We had many a barbecue and I enjoyed incredible hospitality.

Animals in Heaven?

One day, I was informed that we were going to find some kangaroos. I had never seen a kangaroo up close, and as we rocked and rolled in the truck over the uneven terrain, I was excited and hopeful while consciously scanning the horizon, anticipating my first sighting in the wild of one or more of these extraordinary creatures.

Of course, in fact, we weren't in the wild, we were still on the farm but, at its extremities, it felt like we were leaving domesticity behind and going deeper and deeper into the unknown outback. Suddenly my host became animated. He had spotted our first kangaroo. I looked and looked but could see nothing. Without warning, he drew the truck to an abrupt halt and pointed to the ground. "Here she is," he said. It was something of a shock. There on the ground, dead, lay a kangaroo—the first one I'd ever seen in the flesh. She had been hit by a car and had probably died slowly and painfully over many hours, left by the hit-and-run driver to wither and expire. I was confused: on the one hand, I was thrilled to be able to view this amazing creature safely, up close, but I was also devastated that she'd died in such bitterly tragic circumstances. What if she had babies waiting for her somewhere? What if she belonged to a pack and would never again return happily to her family and friends? What had it been like for her to suffer so much in the last hours of her very precious life?

I noticed her pouch, that part of her anatomy that allowed her babies to suckle and to be safe. I noticed her gigantic hind legs, powerful and muscular, and her rather small forelimbs. I was struck by her face: the long, broad nose gave her the appearance of being wise and strong. My host, of course, was not at all fazed by the apparent tragedy of this situation, having seen it many times before, and calmly announced that we would leave her there in order to go and look for a "live one." I was heartbroken. The feelings of grief which I experienced in that moment are as real today as they were then . . .

That kangaroo had just been living her life: going about her existence, gathering food, feeding her babies, bouncing around being a kangaroo, the kangaroo that God had created her to be. Somehow, she had literally clashed with humanity, and it had meant that her life had come to a dismal and harrowing end. Did she not have a right to be the kangaroo that God had created? To jump freely through the plains of Australia? To tend to her babies and belong to her pack? Did she not have, in God, the right to live as God would expect her to live? Just like you and me?

What about the Ethical Treatment of Animals and the Idea of Animal Rights?

We reflect a great deal about human rights today. Humanity has come a long way in understanding that part of honouring the reality and existence of one another, is to honour the right of all humans to, for example, life and liberty, freedom from slavery and torture, freedom of opinion and expression, the right to work and to education . . . and so the list goes on. Catholics and other Christians would naturally go further in the blink of an eye: human beings have these rights because they are created by God, and God himself has dignified humanity with all that it means to be human; indeed we are, among all species, uniquely created in the divine image. Although the world is caught-up in sin and we see the inhumanity of men and women to fellow humans everywhere, in the very core of our being we know that life is sacred and that, as Christians, we want to honour the presence of God in all people, without exception. Surely this principle is summed up by the second great commandment of Jesus: to love your neighbour as yourself (Mark 12:31)?

The Gospel story of the Canaanite woman's faith as told in Matt 15:21–28 is an example of where Jesus models and exemplifies the priority of the individual's rights, especially at a time and in a place where women were not seen to be full members of society. In the story, the woman approaches Jesus and literally begs him to cure her daughter, probably raising her voice in her anxiety and fear. Jesus fails, at first, to respond to the woman, and his disciples tell him that a troublesome woman is wanting to bother him with her request. Mark's version of the story (7:24–30) tells us that Jesus, perhaps understandably, "did not want anyone to know" that he was at the house (7:24). However, eventually, the woman manages to approach Jesus, and falling to her knees, cries: "Lord, help me." Jesus heals her daughter and shows that, by so doing, this Canaanite—an outsider by race, class, and gender—is as worthy of the love and mercy of God as are any (and, by implication, all).

Further, it is said that all the world's major religions have a version of the Golden Rule as found in Jesus: "Whatever you wish that others would do to you, do also to them, for this is the Law and the Prophets" (Matt 7:12). There is a kind of ethical imperative, from a Catholic/Christian perspective, to treat both humans and animals with respect and kindness.

So, who is our neighbour? And what rights might they have, from a Christian perspective? Having accepted that all things in creation are spoken into being by God, and are intended to exist harmoniously and compassionately together, as seen in the opening chapters of the Bible, and as fulfilled in the life and teachings of the Prince of Peace, each species on the planet is very obviously a neighbour to the other. The love and compassion which Jesus shows to the Canaanite woman can be ours to show to all creatures everywhere, at all times. Is this such an odd thing for a Christian to suggest: that God, who is perfect love, and who creates all things out of love and for love, should invite us to live our God-given humanity with dignity and compassion—to fully become what he has created us to be—by respecting, loving, and relating with tenderness to all other humans and all other creatures, of whatever shape or size or species, on the planet? As Andrew Linzey says, "We can't change the world for animals without changing our ideas about animals. We have to move from the idea that animals are things, tools, machines, commodities, resources here for our use, to the idea that as sentient beings they have their own inherent value and dignity."[1] Linzey, an Anglican theologian, drawing on his faith, describes clearly and unequivocally what it means for us, as Christians, to recognise animals as our neighbours, and what changes are necessary in us, and in society, for this Christian principle to be lived authentically. Is that not an obvious response to the love of God which is poured into our hearts through the Holy Spirit (Rom 5:5)?

Regrettably, accidents happen. Tragedy is everywhere. Owing to sin and fallenness, humans fight humans to the death for the right to possess and to control and to own. But there is a greater right. The right to experience freedom to exist without suffering; the right to experience a living-out in an appropriate way the divinely received gifts and talents and mannerisms and ways of being that God has given. Why should this apply only to humans? If we take our vocation to dominion and stewardship of the planet seriously, we surely have the responsibility to respect and honour and uphold and celebrate the rights of all creatures everywhere, human and non-human. This is a fundamental Catholic principle: the sacredness of all life.

Christians naturally want to speak out for the rights of others, in the name of God. We presumably particularly want to protect the rights of those who have no way of advocating for themselves. Animals, as we've already recognised, have no voice of their own, in human terms; they cannot protest when their rights are violated. We need to speak out for them and to ensure that they are accorded all the rights that God offers to them. Animals have rights "in God," we could say, because God has rights. God

---

1. OneKind, "OneKind Talks Animal Ethics," §9.

has the right to expect that animals are treated as he would want them to be treated: with love, with compassion, with kindness, and with the respect that is naturally owed to all that God creates. This is undoubtedly a fundamental Catholic instinct.

Let's return briefly to the catechism. The teaching of the church, as previously mentioned, categorically states that "it is contrary to human dignity to cause animals to suffer or die needlessly."[2] The rights of animals exist because they, like us, find their dignity and their existence in God. Their dignity should be preserved and celebrated because they, in their creaturely fashion, can model to us who God is and what God is like.

A version of the catechism distinctly directed towards young people is specific: "Animals, too, are sentient creatures of God. It is a sin to torture them, allow them to suffer, or to kill them uselessly."[3] All people of good will can naturally resonate with this sentiment. However, some activities and events where animals are used for sport, such as bull fighting or rodeos, appear to contravene this injunction and, thus, the rights-in-God of the animals concerned. It is surprising to us, perhaps, that bull rings in Catholic countries often have chapels attached where Mass is celebrated, a priest is assigned as chaplain, and matadors are blessed. The word "matador" is easily translated as "killer," after all.

Fyodor Dostoyevsky (1821–1881) invites us to reflect further. "Love all of God's creation, the whole of it and every grain of sand. Love every leaf, every ray of God's light! Love the animals, love the plants, love everything! If you love everything, you will perceive the divine mystery in things. And once you have perceived it, you will begin to comprehend it ceaselessly, more and more every day. And you will at last come to love the whole world with an abiding, universal love. Love the animals: God has given them the rudiments of thought and of untroubled joy. Do not, therefore, trouble them, torture them, do not deprive them of their joy, *do not go against God's intent.*"[4]

I learned many things at World Youth Day: I learned that to be in the presence of the Holy Father is absolutely breathtaking; I learned that the Catholic Church is truly universal as I gathered with Catholics from all four corners of the earth; I learned that the gospel imperative to preach Jesus crucified, risen, ascended and glorified must be my life's work. But, perhaps

---

2. *CCC*, §2418.
3. Miller, *YouCat*, §437.
4. Dostoyevsky, *Karamazov,* 167; my emphasis.

surprisingly, my main takeaway memory is of that poor car-crash kangaroo. I will never forget her, nor the compassion with which I related to her death. She opened my heart to the reality of animal suffering and to the ways in which humans can sometimes fail (either accidentally or wilfully) to appropriately share the planet with those whom God has entrusted to us. She changed my heart and gave me a passion to make a difference. I cannot separate my Catholic faith from that beautiful kangaroo; she and my belief in God are intrinsically related: the God whom I worship is the God who creates both me and that beautiful kangaroo. They belong together. She always deserved what God had freely given her, but we took it away.

From Laudato Si', Pope Francis

> Christian thought sees human beings as possessing a particular dignity above other creatures; it thus inculcates esteem for each person and respect for others. Our openness to others, each of whom is a "thou" capable of knowing, loving and entering into dialogue, remains the source of our nobility as human persons. A correct relationship with the created world demands that we not weaken this social dimension of openness to others, much less the transcendent dimension of our openness to the "Thou" of God. Our relationship with the environment can never be isolated from our relationship with others and with God. Otherwise, it would be nothing more than romantic individualism dressed up in ecological garb, locking us into a stifling immanence.[5]

Prayer

Hear our humble prayer, Heavenly Father,
for our friends, the animals,
especially for those who are suffering;
for animals that are overworked, underfed, and cruelly treated;
for all the wistful creatures in captivity, that beat their wings against bars;
for any that are hunted or lost or deserted, or frightened or hungry;
for all that must be put to death.
In the name of Jesus, we entreat for them all your mercy and pity,

---

5. Francis, *LS*, §119.

What about the Ethical Treatment of Animals and the Idea of Animal Rights?

and for those who deal with them,
we ask a heart of compassion and gentle hands and kindly words.
Make us, ourselves,
to be true friends to animals
and so to share the blessings of your never-ending mercy.
Through Jesus Christ our Lord. Amen.

(Traditional prayer)[6]

---

6. Free, *Animals, Nature*, 79.

4

Are There Animals in Heaven?

*I said in my heart with regard to the children of man
that God is testing them, that they may see that they themselves
are but beasts.
For what happens to the children of man and what happens to the
beasts is the same; as one dies, so dies the other.
They all have the same breath, and man has no advantage over the
beasts . . . All go to one place.*
(ECCLESIASTES 3:18–20)

PETER WAS A MAN who was very well-known to me. I saw him every day at Mass. His Catholic faith meant everything to him. In fact, his openness to the things of the Spirit and his desire to live the gospel message of Jesus was edifying and inspiring. I often chatted to Peter after Mass, and we had a friendly way of relating to one another. Truth be told, I admired Peter for his gentle and simple living out of his Catholicism. I wished that I could be more like him.

Peter came from a large Catholic family which went back through many generations, and he could even claim a number of canonised saints among his forebears. He and I often talked about our love for animals and shared funny and moving stories about what our various companion animals and others got up to. His faithful dog Trixie was the absolute love of his life. I kept urging him to bring Trixie to Mass, but he declined. On occasional visits to Peter and his family, I enjoyed the enthusiasm and good spiritedness with which Trixie, a large and loveable Collie, would greet me and any other visitors who happened to be calling. She was everyone's friend. I would often meet Peter and Trixie out on their daily walks in the park and we enjoyed watching our dogs play together and getting up to their usual mischief and tricks.

Sadly, after a period of uncertainty and long-term sickness, Trixie was diagnosed with a terminal illness and her discomfort became very great. The agonising and heartbreaking decision had to be made to end her life. She was suffering so much and in an enormous amount of pain. Ultimately, Peter realised that the last act of love towards his special canine friend was to put her out of that pain, and to allow her to go to sleep peacefully for the final time in his arms. Peter's grief was very real. To say he was devastated would be an understatement. Let's make no mistake about the level of bereavement that animals lovers experience when they lose a beloved companion animal. These animals (of all types and species) become family members, and the feelings of loss and grief are overwhelming. I told Peter that I was praying for him and for his family at this difficult time and that, of course, I would be commending Trixie to God in prayer. God would surely honour the love which was shared between them, I suggested.

I have never had a problem in praying for animals and for their well-being. God has created them to share this planet with us and he hears and answers our prayers for these creatures. St. Catherine of Siena (1347–1380) understood this well: "The reason why God's servants love his creatures so deeply is that they realise how deeply Christ loves them. And this is the very character of love, to love what is loved by those we love."[1]

Some weeks after having had to make the final choice to allow Trixie to die calmly and peacefully in his arms, Peter came to see me. He asked me the inevitable question: will I see Trixie again? Will she be in heaven if I get there? Does her soul have an eternal quality, like a human soul?

These are big questions indeed. Over the years, many scholars and theologians have agonised on just how to address such knotty and challenging issues.

St. Thomas Aquinas (among others) has stated that animals do have souls,[2] but that their soul is significantly different from the human soul.

---

1. Catherine of Siena, *Dialogue*, cited in Linzey and Regan, *Compassion*, 28.
2. Aquinas, *Summa Contra Gentiles*, 4.11

This he refers to as a "sense soul" or a "sensitive soul." Defining what we mean by "soul" seems to be a very particular challenge. Throughout the ages, writers, both Christian and pagan, have used the term to denote all kinds of different understandings and interpretations. In Greek, we hear the word "psyche" used to mean "soul," and in Latin, the word "anima" (so very close to the word "animal") often translated as "soul" or as "life." In this kind of interpretation, scholars seem to be generally referring to that indiscernible yet very real part of an animate (or living, moving) being, and thus setting it apart from an inanimate creature. We know, for example, that a rabbit is different from a tulip. Both are beautiful and both are created by God, but one is a breathing, active creature with feelings of suffering and joy, who has a brain, a nervous system, and some degree of awareness of the world around, whilst the other is noticeably none of these things, yet still remains beautiful and God-created.

Some of the writings in the Bible, especially from the Old Testament, appear to apply the Hebrew term in similar ways at the same time, both to humans and to animals. An example might be the Hebrew phrase *nephesh chayah* (translated as "living soul") to refer both to human beings (as in Gen 2:7) and to animals (Gen 1:30). *Ruach*, the Hebrew word meaning "spirit" or "breath," is applied to both humans and to animals in Eccl 3:21 (as quoted at the head of this chapter). Thinking of "soul" in this broader sense then, we can legitimately believe that animals do have what we might call a soul, because they are alive, filled with the breath of God, and that God has chosen to create them in this way. But is that soul eternal?

Looking at the *Catechism of the Catholic Church* we see very clearly that human beings certainly have a soul, that the soul is intrinsically united to the body, that the soul is immortal, that the soul is a gift from God, and that the soul is often expressed and understood in terms of the heart: the place where ultimate reality exists for all of us, in the depth of our being.[3] The catechism makes no reference at all to the possibility of whether animals have an immortal soul. The church has (perhaps wisely) declined to be decisive about this matter. Many Christians have concluded that animals probably do have a kind of soul, because it is God himself who has breathed life into these creatures. The nature of the soul that animals have, however, is more difficult to define. For Aquinas, it is a life source, an energy which allows movement and engagement with the world. If animals have a soul (of whatever type), then they deserve to experience the life worthy of a

3. *CCC*, §363–68.

God-made creature. If, however, we decide that they don't have a soul, they surely warrant a life worthy of kindness and compassion all the more, because they will have no experience beyond this short, earthly life.

It is logical to see that animals are sentient beings. The UK government declared in April 2022 that the needs of animals must be taken more carefully into account, because they are clearly capable of experiencing suffering. We can see the truth of this simply by observing other creatures. There is a huge difference between an elephant that is left free to be an elephant in the wilds of Africa and the suffering of an elephant isolated, alone, bored, and imprisoned, for example, in a city zoo in the UK; the vast difference between the two is obvious, and we instinctively realise which one is best for the elephant. This sentience, this ability both to suffer and to experience happiness, to have some sort of awareness of the world around them, reminds us of the complexity of how animals experience life. Even if their experience of what it means to be alive is very different to ours, they experience it, nevertheless.

In Rom 8:20–22, St. Paul writes that creation itself will be "set free from slavery to corruption and share in the glorious freedom of the children of God." For St. Paul, there is a sense that the whole of creation is being caught up in the goodness and mercy of God and finding its true identity, its "glorious freedom" (its peaceable kingdom, we might say), through the death and resurrection of Jesus. Animals, of course, are naturally part of this creation. Further, in his Letter to the Ephesians, St. Paul reminds us that the death and resurrection of Jesus has a purpose for all aspects of creation: "In him we have redemption through his blood, the forgiveness of our trespasses, according to the riches of his grace, which he lavished upon us, in all wisdom and insight, making known to us the mystery of his will, according to his purpose, which he set forth in Christ as a plan for the fullness of time, to unite *all things* in him, things in heaven and things on earth" (Eph 1:7–10; my emphasis). All things are drawn together and united in the great Christ-event, after which nothing can ever be the same again (see chapter 6). Humans, animals, plants, and everything in heaven and on earth, are called to share in this destiny, St. Paul seems to be saying.

In a development of this thinking, Paul, in the Letter to the Colossians, remarks, "[Jesus] is the image of the invisible God, the firstborn of *all creation*. For by him, *all things* were created, in heaven and on earth, visible and invisible, whether thrones or dominions or rulers or authorities—*all things* were created through him and for him. . . . For in him all the fullness of God was pleased to dwell, and through him to reconcile to himself *all things*, whether on earth or in heaven, making peace by the blood of his cross" (Col 1:15–17, 19–20; my emphases). The scriptural evidence, especially in these extracts from St. Paul, suggests that the Christ, through whom the whole world was brought into being, is the same Christ whose ministry of reconciliation means that the whole world, in all its various elements and beauty, is brought to fullness and completion, in an ecstatic union of heaven and earth in eternity.

We believe that the death and resurrection of Christ is transformative for the whole of the cosmos, not least the part of creation which we know best, the earth. All sentient creatures are surely capable of experiencing the eternal compassion and peace of the God who first created them. We probably do *not* want to conclude that this love, from an eternal God without beginning or end, is infinite for humans but merely finite for animals; that these animals, as willed members of God's creation, exist only during their earthly life (although this matter is anything but settled among philosophers, theologians, and biblical scholars). We would be free to take such a view, but it seems to me that the God whose love is eternal, and who wants to draw all beings into the perfect community of his everlasting love, at least *allows for the possibility* that all creatures have the potential to live eternally with him in heaven. My cherished Catholic faith leads me to conclude, quite naturally, that God can, and does, consciously will that there is an eternity built into the lives of all animate beings. This does not make animals the same as humans, clearly, but it does allow God the freedom to be God, and to do with his perfect love what he will.

If, as faithful Catholics or Christians of other traditions, we know that God is your creator and mine, and that God is the creator also of animal kind in all its rich variety; and if God loves both us and animals too, then he assuredly intends to restore all of his creatures (us and them) from the bondage that is experienced because of human sin. This is the restored heaven and earth of which the writer of the book of Revelation speaks when God is described as making "*all things* new," surely, and the reestablishment, in Christ, of the peaceable kingdom (Rev 21:1, 5; my emphasis)?

Jesus is, of course, the perfect image of God. When looking to Jesus and his life, we see both the perfection of, and the love of God. Jesus lived the virtues of compassion and mercy and generosity completely perfectly. The gospels reveal him talking about and revealing these virtues again and again—not as ends in themselves, but because they show us the face of the

Father and the power of the Holy Spirit. Is it, perhaps, possible that Jesus would not withhold from animals his loving, redeeming, compassionate love, ordained to bring eternal life to all creation? As the prophet Job tells us, "In [God's] hand is the life of every living thing and the breath of all mankind" (Job 12:10).

Let's return to the peaceable kingdom. Isaiah, in his vision of that city of peace and harmony says that

> the wolf shall dwell with the lamb,
> and the leopard shall lie down with the young goat,
> and the calf and the lion and the fattened calf together;
> and a little child shall lead them.
> The cow and the bear shall graze;
> their young shall lie down together;
> and the lion shall eat straw like the ox.
> The nursing child shall play over the hole of the cobra,
> and the weaned child shall put his hand on the adder's den.
> They shall not hurt or destroy
> in all my holy mountain;
> for the earth shall be full of the knowledge of the Lord
> as the waters cover the sea.
> (Isa 11:6–9)

This passage can be seen to refer to the perfect world which God had originally created and that he intends should last for ever (as we saw in the first chapters of Genesis), while at the same time pointing forward, to a vision of the kingdom when all things are gathered up in the fullness of God's good plan for the world (ultimately, in Jesus Christ—as Jesus himself references in Luke 4:18–21). This is a vision of heaven, a hope of the restoration of all things in Jesus; a place where all the family of the created, in Christ, may "abide in [his] love" and find that their "joy may be full" (John 10:10–11). In this context, we can confidently remind ourselves that God loves all of creation, and that God's love is perfect, so we know that he loves all animals even more than we do. Even if we don't know for sure what happens to animals when they die, we know that it always reflects God's gratuitous and boundless love. That love could surely look like heaven . . .

I remember being on pilgrimage with a group in Fatima, Portugal, in 2010. We had already planned to travel there before we realised that Pope Benedict would be present at the same time. It was an added blessing to share that sacred place of pilgrimage with the Holy Father. One evening, it was announced that Pope Benedict would lead the rosary for any who wanted to join him. I quickly gathered up my things and, with rosary in pocket, set off for the sanctuary. Fatima is a shrine that receives upwards of five million pilgrims a year so, with the attendance of the pope, there were what felt like at least that many there! By some happy blessing, I found myself seated at the very front of the rows of priests who had gathered. It was so moving to be with the successor of St. Peter as he prayed the prayer he must have uttered so very many times throughout his life. As a lover of the rosary, I felt an instant connection to Pope Benedict, who was kneeling just a few feet away from me as we recited, in many different tongues, but united in the language of prayer, those familiar words from Luke's Gospel, "Hail Mary, full of grace . . ." (Luke 1:28). As so often happens with prayer (perhaps mostly when we don't even acknowledge or notice it), the reality of heaven and the perfection of God broke through, uniting each of us to one another and to Our Lady. It was a beautiful, touching moment. Heaven resonated on earth. As much as I felt that I could reach out and touch the pope—so, too, heaven had reached out and touched us.

With these thoughts, I suggest that heaven is at least a possibility for animals (as well as for you and for me) and that we will, please God, one day hope to share this perfect state in eternity with all of God's creation. Even if we conclude that animals do not have souls in the way that we humans do, we can certainly see, looking at the biblical evidence (especially in Rom 8:20–22 and Eph 1:9–10), that it is the intention and will of God the Father to unite *all things* in Jesus, things in heaven and things on earth. By the power of Christ's saving work, each element of creation finds its wholeness and destiny in Jesus. That, to me, suggests very strongly that animals could, with us, share in the glory of eternal life with Jesus.

The poet Alfred Lord Tennyson (1809–1892) senses the power and love of the God who excludes nothing that he has created:

> Oh yet we trust that something good
> will be the final goal of ill,
> to pangs of nature, sins of will,
> defects of doubt and taints of blood;
> That nothing walks with aimless feet,
> that not one life shall be destroy'd,
> or cast as rubbish to the void,
> when God hath made the pile complete.[4]

---

4. Tennyson, *In Memoriam*, §54.

Remembering Peter and Trixie, Peter himself, some months after Trixie died, came to experience his own death. His dying was peaceful and he was strengthened by the love of his family and the sacraments of the church for his final journey. When it came to planning his funeral Mass, Peter's son took me to one side and, with some embarrassment, told me that he hoped I would accommodate a particular request for the family. His father had left very clear instructions that Trixie's ashes should be buried with Peter in the same plot of ground. I, of course, immediately understood this sentiment and readily agreed. Why wouldn't these two loving companions share a unity in death, as they had in life? What's more, it seemed to me entirely acceptable to happily trust and to pray that they could, perhaps, be together again in heaven.

From Laudato Si', Pope Francis

> As Christians, we are called "to accept the world as a sacrament of communion, as a way of sharing with God and our neighbours on a global scale. It is our humble conviction that the divine and the human meet in the slightest detail in the seamless garment of God's creation, in the last speck of dust of our planet."[5]
> (Quoting Patriarch Bartholomew of Constantinople)

Prayer

Lord, make me an instrument of your peace.
Where there is hatred, let me sow love;
where there is injury, pardon;
where there is doubt, faith;
where there is despair, hope;
where there is darkness, light;
and where there is sadness, joy.

O Divine Master, grant that I may not so much seek
to be consoled as to console;
to be understood as to understand;
to be loved as to love.

5. Francis, *LS*, §9.

For it is in giving that we receive;
it is in pardoning that we are pardoned;
and it is in dying that we are born to eternal life.
[For you, Jesus, are Lord, for ever and ever.]
Amen.

(Sometimes attributed to St. Francis of Assisi)[6]

---

6. "Peace Prayer."

5

Can Animals Teach Us Anything about Our Faith and about Our Belief in God?

The King will say to those on his right,
"Come you who are blessed by my Father,
inherit the kingdom prepared for you from the foundation of the world."

(MATTHEW 25:34)

My sheep hear my voice, and I know them, and they follow me.
(JOHN 10:27)

I COMPLETELY BLAME PEPE, my beloved cockapoo, for an ever-deepening fascination with animals and for the very real concern that I have for their well-being. Indeed, I'd dare to say that Pepe has turned me into something of an animal advocate and taught me more than I could ever have imagined.

I remember Pepe as an eight-week-old puppy. I could hold him in the palm of my hand. When first I brought him home, he couldn't manage the stairs, and I had to carry him in my arms up to bed at night. I had not wanted to contact a breeder in order to give Pepe a home, and instead had approached one of the large national dog-homing rescue charities. Somehow, they didn't seem very interested in me, and I ended up, instead of rescuing a homeless dog, accepting Pepe from a professional breeder, who acquired financial gain from me as a result. Now, knowing so much more about the many homeless and unloved dogs out there, I wouldn't even consider going to a breeder but, instead, would always rescue. At the time I met Pepe, I hadn't worked all of this out. Subsequently Georgie, and then Lady Grace (no longer with me), came from a very reputable and outstanding charity.

We grew up with animals in the family home. They were always around. My mother brought us up on her own and, despite the extra challenges that animals must have given (while she, at one stage, held down three different jobs simultaneously), she always saw the value of allowing dogs, cats, rabbits, and goldfish to share our lives. I am so grateful for that. I remember, especially, Jason the stunning black Labrador with an insatiable appetite, and Sooty, the kitten with the beautiful silk-velvet coat.

Once I left home, first to go to music college and then to seminary, animals couldn't really be in the picture. I shared my living spaces with others and anyway finances were always very sparse. After being ordained, I threw myself into my ministry and nothing would stop me from whizzing around the parish like a success-crazed entrepreneur. I loved the pastoral work, and I loved celebrating Mass; hearing confessions was a joy, and visiting the sick in hospital and at home energised me and gave me a deep sense of having found the niche in life for which I believe God has created me. At that stage, I had no time for anything other than being the very best priest that I could. Looking back, I recognise that I was rather unhealthily driven to achieve and to be seen to be successful (whatever that might mean in terms of the priesthood).

Earlier in my life, I had been through what can only be described as significant ongoing trauma over a period of many years. I had pushed these repeated dark experiences to the back of my heart and had (apparently successfully) tried to somehow heal myself by rushing around healing everyone else. In a way, it was a very fruitful (if subconscious) technique: all the time I was looking out for others, I didn't need to look out for myself.

Some forty-five years later, and now a parish priest living alone, a very weighty pastoral encounter significantly triggered every last bit of that trauma, and alarmingly sent me straight back to those gloomy, painful days. It was a total and complete shock, and I hadn't expected it—after all, I had lived for decades with memories and flashbacks, and with a veil over my heart that I subsequently carried as a result of those experiences. Suddenly I found myself back in the midst of it all, along with the suffering that went with it. This is not the place to unpack the psychology and science of the very real trauma through which I was going, but it is enough to say that eventually I felt able to share this reality with close friends, a trauma therapist, and a wise spiritual director. With their support, I decided that a canine companion would help me to heal.

For years, people had seen me at work in the parishes in which I had been placed and said things like "you can't possibly have a dog, you're never at home!" or "how will you find time to walk a dog in the middle of your busy schedule?" or "you're a bachelor who likes your way of doing things, are you not a little too selfish to share your time and energies with a dog?" and so on. I had listened and, knowing that they usually had my best interests at heart, had reckoned that they were probably right. I still regret my decision not to have a canine companion sooner.

Eventually I found Pepe (and he found me) and I can say, in all honesty, that my life was changed. With Pepe I had a real emotional connection and, in a profound way, he taught me to love myself again. For years, the trauma with which I had lived had shut me down (not that I would have showed it), and suddenly my heart was opening again. This little bundle of fun and joy was healing me; actually healing me. In loving Pepe so very much and, in time, Georgie and Grace too, I somehow learned to love *me* again. Pepe showed me how to slowly heal from the old self-critical fraud that I had inwardly become, always firmly believing that I was, deep down, a failure and an imposter. Instead, he drew me into becoming more gentle and tender both with myself and with my feelings, and in the ways in which I engaged with ordinary life. In connecting more deeply, for the first time in my life, with Pepe, I connected in a new and more profound way with me. It is an extraordinary thing that it took me so long to learn this lesson, and that it was a little loveable crossbreed dog who showed me the truth. In loving my dogs and, by extension, all animals, I learned so much about the power and strength of human love and especially about the command to love myself (Mark 12:31), because of my new awareness that I (and the whole of creation) was loved by God: "As the Father has loved me," says Jesus, "so I have loved you. Abide in my love" (John 15:9). I was reminded, in a new and startling way, of the truth of that beautiful passage which I heard so frequently proclaimed at funeral Masses: "Who shall separate us from the love of Christ? Shall tribulation, or distress, or persecution? . . . In all these things we are more than conquerors through him who loved us" (Rom 8:35, 37). And all because of a little black dog.

My story is just that: my story (well, that part of it, anyway). Each of us will have our own experiences on which to draw and which shape and fashion us throughout our lives. In Luke 13:34, Jesus says, "O Jerusalem, Jerusalem, killing the prophets and stoning those who are sent to you! How often would I have gathered your children together as a hen gathers her brood under her wings, and you would not!" Jesus appears to be suggesting, in these words, that he is frustrated by the way that we humans, entrusted with so much by God, can treat one another. It is so easy to be judgmental and critical and unkind. But, says Jesus, he wants to nurture us and to sustain us, just as a mother hen protects and cares for her vulnerable brood of chicks. It is clear that the maternal instinct is very evident in the world of animals. All species, without exception, have a God-given, inbuilt desire to safeguard and sustain their young. We could even say that this reality is written into the very way in which God invites us to experience the world; it's one of the means which God uses to help us to see something of his loving will and purpose for us and for all creatures.

Some years ago, I helped to lead a pilgrimage to the Holy Land. As well as visiting many holy sites and following in the footsteps of Jesus, we pilgrims were able to experience the land of the Bible in a tangible way. Everywhere we went we were besieged by pedlars and tradesmen and workers, each trying to earn a day's living. Donkeys and camels abounded. I remember on one occasion seeing a poor, terrified donkey loaded up with such a huge heavy weight of bricks that he could barely walk. I was horrified to see the donkey's guardian beating him with a stick to make him take a further painful step forward. I also recall with shame how I watched a member of our group, like a tourist, take a ride on a camel. Again, the camel was hit repeatedly with a stick and pulled about by a head-rope to force her to do what her trainer wanted. We all watched and laughed and took out our cameras in order to capture the amusing moment of our fellow pilgrim parading around on the back of that poor camel. I'm sorry to say that I laughed and clapped along with the rest of them.

Treating animals in this heartless and exploitative way just commodifies them and encourages humans to see them as mere objects and not as the living, sentient, loving creatures that they are born to be. I still feel ashamed for participating so enthusiastically in that spectacle. I did not behave in a loving way to that creature of God. Let that be a lesson to me.

I have come to see that nothing gives me the right to use any of God's creatures in this way. If you like, looking back at those two examples, I realise that I must choose, in all my relations with humans and with animals, kindness rather than cruelty, and respect rather than contempt. The choice is mine to make, not just because kindness and respect are better than cruelty or contempt (though, of course they are), but because they are the virtues that I see modelled in the life of Jesus (healing the sick, feeding the hungry, teaching those around him, caring for the widow, defending the children and so on), and in the compassion to which the Scriptures call me: "Be kind and compassionate to one another, forgiving each other, just as in Christ, God forgave you" (Eph 4:32). In Mark 1:41, Jesus, "moved with pity," stretches out his hand to heal the leper. I wonder what more I could be doing, day by day, to "heal" the donkey, the camel, and all the other animals that have crossed my path throughout my life, and will continue to do so?

St. John Chrysostom (347–407), in a powerful homily, presents a challenge to all who dare to call themselves Christians and to live a Christlike life: "Holy people are most loving and gentle in their dealings with others, and even with the lower animals: for this reason it was said that 'A righteous man is merciful to the life of his beasts.' (*Proverbs 12:10*) Surely we ought to show kindness and gentleness to animals for many reasons, and chiefly because they are of the same origin as ourselves?"[1] In seeing Jesus in his creation, and even in the lives and loves of our companion (and other) animals, we are better able to seek, find, and love Jesus within ourselves.

Socrates (470–399 BC), the Greek philosopher, famously said that "vice harms the doer."[2] Long before the gospels and the life and teaching of Jesus of Nazareth, this wise man of the ancient world recognised that when violence is used to intentionally harm another, that same violence is equally detrimental to the well-being of the one inflicting the harm. Somehow, we become less than who God has created us to be when we live a life of violence and when we inflict suffering on others. Violence, like all sins, can become habitual and, with St. Paul, we can say that "I do not understand my own actions. For I do not do what I want, but I do the very thing that I hate" (Rom 7:15).

---

1. John Chrysostom, "Homilies," cited in Linzey and Regan, *Compassion*, 65.
2. Cited in White, *Discovering Philosophy*, 331.

There is a wealth of evidence available online (and elsewhere) today to show how much intentional violence and harm is done to animals. Innocent creatures who just want to live are treated as objects in CAFOs (Contained Animal Feeding Units) throughout the world, and little thought is given to their natural needs. In the UK, for example, despite a call from the Farm Animal Welfare Council as far back as 2003, and a promise from the government to end the practice, pigs are still slaughtered with an excessive use of CO_2. This causes the terrified pigs extreme suffering and, sadly, a fairly slow, painful death.[3]

As a Catholic Christian, who believes that the teachings of Jesus Christ are the answer to every question that we shall ever ask, I cannot condone the killing of pigs (just one example of many, regrettably) in this way, given that so much harm and suffering is caused—but, I have to say too, that my pastoral heart is also enormously concerned for the men and women who are causing this intentional violence. What must such regular, horrific killing, apparently normalised, do to the hearts and souls of these precious people? My duty, as a priest and as a teacher of the faith, is to say that this way of living cannot be consistent with a compassionate, pro-life ethic, whether directed towards humans or towards animals.

In 2021, Nick Palmer, head of Compassion in World Farming UK, wrote that "the suffering pigs experience when slaughtered using carbon dioxide is [a] real scandal. Every year, millions of British pigs are facing terrible treatment at slaughter, killed using CO_2. This method involves lowering pigs into a CO_2 chamber, where they panic, fight for breath and eventually suffocate. It can take as long as sixty seconds for them to lose consciousness. The truth is that CO_2 killing of pigs is as much non-stun slaughter as simply cutting an animal's throat and letting them bleed to death. In both cases, animals experience a prolonged period of pain, suffering and distress. This awful cruelty has to end. It's high time the UK Government took action to end this suffering by fully funding research to find humane alternatives to this severe welfare problem that has existed since the mid-1990s."[4]

We are invited, by saint and scholar alike, to think carefully about our relationship with animals and to celebrate who they are as God's gift to us and to the whole of creation. Thomas à Kempis (ca. 1418–1427) writes in his famous *The Imitation of Christ*, "If your heart be right, then every

3. UK Farm Animal Welfare Council, *Report*.
4. "UK Government."

created thing will become for you a mirror of life and a book of holy teaching. For there is nothing created so small and mean that it does not reflect the goodness of God."[5]

God's way is not the way of exploitation and arrogant control, but a way of compassion and service and love. It is more than possible that God has blessed the earth with animals to teach us about how to be better human beings, human beings who love unconditionally like Jesus, and to remember that each and every human, and each and every animal, is precious in God's sight.

From Laudato Si', Pope Francis

> The world, created according to the divine model, is a web of relationships. Creatures tend towards God, and in turn it is proper to every living being to tend towards other things, so that throughout the universe we can find any number of constant and secretly interwoven relationships. This leads us not only to marvel at the manifold connections existing among creatures, but also to discover a key to our own fulfilment. The human person grows more, matures more and is sanctified more to the extent that he or she enters into relationships, going out from themselves to live in communion with God, with others and with all creatures.[6]

Prayer

Blessed are you, Lord our God, for you have made all things well. You have given us innocent companions on our life journey; animals wild and tame. They are wonderful in all their variety of shapes, sizes, and abilities. We marvel at their beauty, which draws us closer to you who made them. Keep them thriving and able to carry out what your law intends for them. Let us never see them as only for trade or profit, but always as creatures of your wisdom. Bless these animals with us now, and all the creatures throughout your good earth. We ask this through Christ our Lord. Amen.

(From Catholic Rural Life)[7]

---

5. Kempis, *Imitation*, 67.
6. Francis, *LS*, §240.
7. Catholic Rural Life, "October," §25.

6

Does the Resurrection of Jesus Make a Difference for Animals?

Your righteousness is like the mountains of God;
your judgements are like the great deep;
man and beast you save, O Lord.

(P*SALM* 36:6)

[Christ] is the image of the invisible God, the firstborn of all creation. For by him all things were created, in heaven and on earth, visible and invisible, whether thrones or dominions or rulers or authorities—all things were created through him and for him. And he is before all things, and in him all things hold together. . . . In him, all the fullness of God was pleased to dwell, and through him to reconcile to himself all things, whether in earth or in heaven, making peace by the blood of his cross.

(C*OLOSSIANS* 1:15–17, 10–20)

I HAD ONLY BEEN in the parish a few days before Jim rang to introduce himself and his wife, Mary. An elderly couple from the north of England, they were faithful Catholics and keen for the new parish priest to call in and say hello. Sadly, infirmity and frailty meant that getting to Mass was impossible for them now, and they relied on home visits from the priest and the people. They were well known to many parishioners and were respected, by all who knew them, for their valued place within the parish community.

Just a few weeks after that first visit, the phone rang at about 2:30 a.m. The loud, shrill tone aggressively forced me awake and I sleepily mumbled a greeting. "Father, it's Jim," I heard, "please come as soon as you can. It's Mary. I think she has died. The police and the medics are on their way." Ever grateful for the accuracy of the satnav, I drove through the dark night to find the house once again. The police car was parked outside, and I tentatively approached the front door. Mary had already died and was still lying on the bedroom floor. Two very young police officers were waiting with Jim and providing comfort and support. He was, of course, glad to see me and I was pleased to help and reassure him.

They were the perfectly suited couple: never apart; always together; finishing one another's sentences and complementing one another in so many ways. Jim was naturally devastated. "Is there anything you can do for Mary, Father?" he asked. I explained that I would pray for Mary and say the special blessings and prayers reserved for those who had suddenly died. Mary had, indeed, breathed her last, and I was honoured to go to her and minister to her as I had been ordained to do. A regular communicant, and a devout person of prayer, this was the very least that the church could (and should) do for Mary, and I was privileged to be the priest who was there at the time. Jim became increasingly distressed, and I spent the rest of that night, after the police had left, with him, praying with him, chatting with him, and reassuring him. We drank many cups of tea. As day broke, I was able to call members of the parish St. Vincent de Paul group, who kindly came and sat with Jim, allowing me the opportunity to leave and to prepare for that morning's Mass.

While we were chatting, Jim was asking me about heaven and our Christian hope of eternal life. "I've always wondered," he said, "if the power of Christ to save me and you and my beloved Mary is actually greater than we realise."

"How do you mean, Jim?" I asked.

"Well, we talk, don't we, about everything having been changed by the power of the death and resurrection of Jesus, and that, because of that event, nothing can ever be the same again?" Jim had been well catechised and knew the teachings of the church and his Catholic faith well. "Does that mean that every aspect of creation, even the parts that we cannot see, is caught up in the redeeming work of Christ?"

Jesus is, of course, a historical figure who lived here on earth, as decreed by the eternal will of God the Father. He existed in time and space, and even many sceptics accept the historical evidence that Jesus of Nazareth lived and moved in the territories of Palestine for around thirty-three years in the first century. For Christians, he was/is a great teacher, an amazing miracle-worker, and an incredible moral exemplar. However, he is also, much more importantly, for those who believe, the Saviour, the incarnate Son of God: the One who, according to the loving will of the Father, dies so that sins may be forgiven, hurts can be healed, and hopes fulfilled, thus offering the very real promise of eternal life. But, if I may put it this way, he is even more than that. The Word, having existed before the beginning of time, is part of the very fabric of God's ongoing creating and sustaining of the world, of the whole of the created order. As testified by the Scriptures, Jesus of Nazareth, born of the womb of the Blessed Virgin, the Word become flesh (John 1:14), is an eternal reality existing within and without the structure and fabric of creation. He is the pattern by whom the universe has been conceived, continues to exist, and is being constantly upheld and sustained. This is the Jesus, who "in the beginning was the Word, and the Word was with God, and the Word was God. He was in the beginning with God. All things were made through him, and without him was not anything made that was made. In him was life" (John 1:1–4).

The Jesus of the cosmos, the Jesus who acts to redeem the entirety of all things created by God, is the Jesus who was there when the world was created; he is, as we say every week in the creed, God from God, Light from Light, true God from true God, through whom all things were made. This is the Jesus who reconciles all things to himself and makes peace for all things by the blood of his cross (Col 1:20).

Despite the years of human-centred teaching suggesting that animals are here for us to use as we wish and that, if necessary, their suffering is permitted, this element of Christ's reign and authority cannot be overlooked. If, in his death and resurrection, Jesus gathers to himself all created things, then it certainly seems possible that he brings nearer to his divine heart all creatures, human and animal, in his saving work; that the full and complete diversity of the cosmos, in all of its parts, is open to the potential of being redeemed, raised, and restored by the Lord of Life.

Does the Resurrection of Jesus Make a Difference for Animals?

In *Laudato Si'*, connecting Christ's real presence in the Mass with the elements of Christ's overarching and redeeming work, Pope Francis (referring to previous comments from Pope Benedict XVI) emphatically exclaims, "Indeed the Eucharist is itself an act of cosmic love: 'Yes, cosmic! Because even when it is celebrated on the humble altar of a country church, the Eucharist is always in some way celebrated on the altar of the world.' The Eucharist joins heaven and earth; it embraces and penetrates all creation. The world which came forth from God's hands returns to him in blessed and undivided adoration: in the bread of the Eucharist, 'creation is projected towards divinisation, towards the holy wedding feast, towards unification with the creator himself.'"[1]

This idea is mind-blowing and one, perhaps, that we rarely consider. If we take it seriously and, for the sake of both humans and animals, it is good that we should, it means that Jesus is Lord of the past, the present, and the future; that he is not just the root and source of all spirituality and morality but, rather, the foundation too of physics, chemistry, biology and all the sciences, arts, and varying aspects of life (including cosmology and everything else in creation).

The *Catechism of the Catholic Church* is clear that "nothing exists that does not owe its existence to God the creator. The world began when God's word drew it out of nothingness; *all existent beings, all of nature,* all human history is rooted in this primordial event, the very genesis by which the world was constituted, and time begun."[2] That, to me, sounds pretty conclusive and, in terms of Christ's redeeming work, suggests that nothing created by God is likely to be left out of the ambit and scope of that power and love at the end of time.

The view of all things being gathered up in the death and resurrection of Christ is further emphasised in the catechism, which declares that all creatures "have the same creator" and that they are "all ordered to his glory."[3] All things, animal, fish, human, the planets, the earth, the plants, the seas, the stars, are ordered and drawn to the glory of God, finding their meaning and purpose in the once-for-all Christ-event.

> Most high, all powerful, all good Lord!
> All praise is yours, all glory, all honour, and all blessing.

---

1. Francis, *LS*, §236.
2. *CCC*, §338; my emphasis.
3. *CCC*, §344.

> To you, alone, Most High, do they belong. No mortal lips are worthy to pronounce your name.
> Be praised, my Lord, through all your creatures,
> especially through my lord Brother Sun, who brings the day;
> and you give light through him.
> And he is beautiful and radiant in all his splendour!
> Of you, Most High, he bears the likeness.
> Be praised, my Lord, through Sister Moon and the stars;
> in the heavens you have made them, precious and beautiful.
> Be praised, my Lord, through Brothers Wind and Air,
> and clouds and storms, and all the weather,
> through which you give your creatures sustenance.
> Be praised, My Lord, through Sister Water;
> she is very useful, and humble, and precious, and pure.
> Be praised, my Lord, through Brother Fire,
> through whom you brighten the night.
> He is beautiful and cheerful, and powerful and strong.
> Be praised, my Lord, through our sister Mother Earth,
> who feeds us and rules us and produces various fruits with coloured flowers and herbs.
> Be praised, my Lord, through those who forgive for love of you;
> through those who endure sickness and trial.
> Happy those who endure in peace, for by you,
> Most High, they will be crowned.
> Be praised, my Lord, through our Sister Bodily Death,
> from whose embrace no living person can escape. . . .
> Praise and bless my Lord, and give thanks,
> and serve him with great humility.[4]

The "Canticle of the Creatures" of St. Francis does not specifically mention animals, as is clear to see, but refers to "all creatures," and consciously places those creatures within the context of the whole of creation. It is, after all, the plan and desire of the creator to make known to us "the mystery of his will, according to his purpose, which he set forth in Christ, as a plan for the fullness of time, to unite all things in him, things in heaven and things on earth" (Eph 1:10).

The purpose for which humans and animals are created, as I have suggested previously, includes the unstoppable and irrepressible goodness and love of God: he creates because, in doing so, his love cannot contain itself and expresses itself in goodness, in the world, in animals, and in humans. The bringing all of that goodness together through the death and

---

4. Francis of Assisi, "Canticle of the Creatures," §1–4.

resurrection of Christ has been God's plan and his dream since before creation itself and following the fall and the original sin of the man and the woman in the garden.

In the peaceable kingdom, as seen in both the Old and New Testaments, God creates all things to be in union and fellowship with him; in the new covenant, established through the saving work of Jesus, he chooses, in love, that the entirety of creation be one with him again. It is a moment of graced election; God cannot but be filled with desire for every aspect of creation, in all its glorious difference and splendour, to be reunited with him, bringing about (in Jesus) reconciliation and renewal for humans, animals, and all other created things.

Pope Benedict speaks about the cosmic influence of the death and resurrection of Jesus and, in a homily on priesthood and the Mass from 2009, says, "The role of the priesthood is to consecrate the world so that it may become a living Host, a liturgy: so that the liturgy may not be something alongside the reality of the world, but that the world itself shall become a living Host, a liturgy. This is also the great vision of Teilhard de Chardin: in the end we shall achieve a true cosmic liturgy, where the cosmos becomes a living Host."[5] The great pope sees no distinction between the different elements of creation, but rather that, in Christ, all parts of God's good creation will be caught up in the cosmic liturgy which is the Christ-event, and in which humans and animals and all aspects of the created order share. These reflections of Pope Benedict XVI are offered, of course, not just to priests, but to all Catholics and other Christians; indeed to all who share in the labour of proclaiming the gospel, and who are called to offer the world to God, and to find sanctification through their ordinary life and work.

The Jesuit Pierre Teilhard de Chardin (1881–1955) was a French priest, scientist, palaeontologist, theologian, philosopher, and teacher. His theological views have presented a challenge to some, who question his Catholic orthodoxy. It is, therefore, all the more extraordinary that the pope should feel so compelled to use these words.

The passage to which Benedict XVI refers comes from de Chardin's book, *Hymn of the Universe* (published posthumously).[6] Like many priests, de Chardin chose to celebrate Mass every day. On one occasion, finding himself in the middle of the Ordos desert in China, while on a scientific expedition, he realised that to offer the Mass would be impossible. Instead,

---

5. Benedict XVI, "Homily," §14.
6. Chardin, *Hymn*, 17.

he wrote a heartfelt prayer exploring, in poetic prose, the sacredness of all creation, reflecting on the simplicity, coherence, and harmony of all things in Jesus, the King of Heaven and Earth, the gatherer-up of all things, the genesis and the fulfilment from which, and to which, all parts of the cosmos tend. In effect, it is a kind of eucharistic prayer in the absence of bread and wine and, instead, is celebrated on the "altar" of the whole universe. Entitled "The Mass on the World," he prays, "I, your priest, will make the whole earth my altar and on it will offer you all the labours and sufferings of the world," and "all the things in the world to which this day will bring increase; all those that will diminish; all those too that will die: all of them, Lord, I try to gather into my arms, so as to hold them out to you in offering." He continues (in what is a very long prayer) by saying, "You know how your creatures can come into being only, like shoot from stem, as part of an endlessly renewed process," and "you who gather into your exuberant unity every beauty, every affinity, every energy, every mode of existence; it is you to whom my being cried out with a desire as vast as the universe, 'In truth you are my Lord and my God.'"[7]

De Chardin is moved to consider the way in which Jesus is both already restoring and rebuilding his broken world but how, at the same time, that fragmented universe still awaits its transformation into the new heaven and new earth of which we read in the last book of the Bible (Rev 21:1), and which is brought to completion through, with, and in Christ, the Alpha and Omega, the beginning and the end (Rev 21:6). With Pope Benedict, I find de Chardin's prayer powerful and uplifting—beautiful, even—but mostly it reveals to me the potential for animals that God has given in restoring all things in Christ (see Acts 3:21), as he gathers into his "exuberant unity every beauty . . . every mode of existence."

Another Jesuit, Robert Murray (1926–2018), focusses on the peaceable kingdom in the context of Christ's death and resurrection. In his *The Cosmic Covenant*, Murray presents much well-researched scriptural analysis to show the glory of the coming of the messianic kingdom, a kingdom in which all will be called to the side of Christ for eternity. He draws attention to the importance of the vision of Isa 11:6–9, as a prophecy of the peaceable kingdom which is God's will for his creation. He reminds us that a very similar passage appears again, later in Isaiah, recalling the power of a place where harmony and peace can reign: "The wolf and the lamb shall graze together; the lion shall eat straw like the ox. . . . They shall not

---

7. Chardin, *Hymn*, 132–33.

hurt or destroy in all my holy mountain" (Isa 65:25).⁸ God's dream for his kingdom, already being achieved through the death and resurrection of Jesus, will turn enmities on their head and draw enemies into friendship. Even predatory animals will come to eat straw and live in gentleness with their former prey.

Pope John Paul II has also given some time to reflecting on this important matter. He says that our service to creation is "ministerial . . . a real reflection of the unique and infinite lordship of God," which he invites us all to exercise "with wisdom and love."⁹ Pope Benedict refers to worship, in his book *Spirit of the Liturgy*, as the "soul of the covenant" that "not only saves mankind but is also meant to draw the whole of reality into communion with God."¹⁰ Again, all beings are, for both popes, caught up in the universal saving work of Jesus who draws the whole of reality into eternity.

More recently, in *Laudato Si'*, Pope Francis has challenged us to be "instruments of God our Father, so that our planet might be what he desired when he created it and correspond with his plan for peace, beauty and fullness."¹¹ "The ultimate destiny of the universe is in the fullness of God," he says, "which has already been attained by the risen Christ, the measure of the maturity of all things. . . . The ultimate purpose of other creatures," says the Holy Father, "is not to be found in us. Rather, all creatures are moving forward with us and through us towards a common point of arrival, which is God, in that transcendent fullness where the risen Christ embraces and illumines all things. Human beings, endowed with intelligence and love, and drawn by the fullness of Christ, are called to lead all creatures back to their Creator."¹² There we have it. Pope Francis sums it up beautifully. In speaking of the value of human dominion and stewardship of the planet, the pope puts it in the context of the eternal, and in the heart of Jesus, risen, ascended and glorified, where the resurrection of Jesus embraces and illumines all things. After all, "[Christ] offered blood to God to cleanse the *entire world*."¹³

---

8. Also see v. 27 onwards, for a fuller example.
9. John Paul II, *Evangelium Vitae*, §52.
10. Ratzinger, *Spirit of the Liturgy*, 27.
11. Francis, *LS*, §53.
12. Francis, *LS*, §83.
13. Nazianzen, *On the Son: Selected Poems*, cited in Linzey and Regan, *Compassion*, 81; my emphasis.

The theologian F. D. Maurice (1805–1872) speaks movingly of these truths: "Thank [God] because he has said there will be a day in which he will gather up all things unto Christ, both things in heaven and things on earth, unto him who is the head over all his universe; and when every child, and every star, and every animal, and every flower, shall be seen to have been created by infinite love for his infinite glory."[14]

In *All God's Animals: A Catholic Theological Framework for Animal Ethics*, Christopher Steck, SJ, reminds us that "in the liturgy, the Christian community participates in this work by drawing creation into the event of its salvation. In offering the earthly elements of bread and wine, the church lifts up all creation to the Father and joins the voices of creation in a grateful eucharistic praise."[15] It is not beyond the mind of God, or of his church, to bring animals and all aspects of creation to the fullness of completion and joy in Jesus Christ. This, indeed, is God's plan for the world.

Laudato Si', Pope Francis

> God is ultimately present to each being, without impinging on the autonomy of his creature. . . . His divine presence, which ensures the subsistence and growth of each being, "continues the work of creation." The Spirit of God has filled the universe with possibilities and therefore, from the very heart of things, something new can always emerge. "Nature is nothing other than a certain kind of art, namely God's art, impressed upon things . . ."[16]

Prayer

Heavenly Father, Creator of all that is good and beautiful in this world, we come before you in humble prayer, asking for your protection and care for the natural world that you have created. From the mountains to the oceans, from the forests to the deserts, your hand has formed and moulded this world to be a place of wonder and majesty. And yet, in our own ignorance and selfishness, we have caused harm to your creation. We ask for your mercy and grace upon all the creatures of the earth, from the smallest insect

---

14. Maurice, *Sermons*, cited in Linzey and Regan, *Compassion*, 84.
15. Steck, *All God's Animals*, 164.
16. Francis, *LS*, §80, quoting St. Thomas Aquinas.

to the mightiest elephant. May they live in peace, free from fear and suffering, and may their habitat be protected and preserved for generations to come. We pray for the oceans and the rivers, for the air and the soil, that they may be purified and refreshed, and that your creation may flourish once again. We ask for your guidance and wisdom as we work to heal the planet, that we may be good stewards of all that you have entrusted to us. And may we learn to live in harmony with all creatures and with the earth, that your love and peace may reign in all the world. We make this prayer through Jesus Christ our Lord. Amen.

(From richoffaith.com)[17]

---

17. Written by Federico Angiolini (Rich Offaith). Used with permission.

7

What about Animals and the Holy Mass?

"Behold, the Lamb of God, who takes away the sins of the world!"
"I saw the Spirit descend from heaven like a dove,
and it remained on him."

(JOHN 1:29, 32)

I HAVE ALWAYS FELT very drawn to the celebration of the Mass. During my youth, I longed for the opportunity to engage with the Mass as a priest. I have discovered that, when I'm stood at the altar celebrating Mass, this is the very place where I'm meant to be. My sense of vocation is clarified, deepened and reinforced every time I share in this beautiful liturgical experience.

I have celebrated Mass in all kinds of places and situations and, different as they all are, the joy of priesthood and the profound connection between priesthood and the Mass always fills me with wonder and awe. Why God would choose me—yes, me—for this incredible calling is a question best not asked. I must leave that to God and to his divine plan.

It was whilst at the Royal College of Music as an undergraduate that my vocation grew. I arrived there in South Kensington, knowing that God was probably calling me to the priesthood, and I was very open to that possibility, but my love of music wouldn't go away, and I had a fabulous time with my fellow musicians (many of whom are now household names in the world of classical music), experiencing the art of music-making to the highest possible standard. God speaks through music. God speaks though art. God continued, at that time, to speak to me and to call me to the altar as a priest.

Of course, music and priesthood go very well together. A priest who can sing is able to bring the gift of music to the liturgy and, especially, to the Mass. So as a musician and as a priest, I find myself inhabiting the right space when I celebrate Mass. I often remind my parishioners, in encouraging them to raise their voices in praise, of St. Augustine of Hippo's famous axiom that those who sing well pray twice, and that "singing is for the one who loves."[1]

The Mass always revitalises and refreshes. I remember the telephone ringing at about 4 a.m. one morning. It was a call from the hospital. Could I come now, as a family wanted their beloved relative to receive the Last Rites? As I hauled myself out of bed, I wondered, for a moment, whether I really wanted to go out at such a time on a wet, cold night in deep November. But go I did. I was at the bedside of the patient for an hour or two as I celebrated the Sacrament of the Sick, said the Apostolic Blessing/Absolution, and prayed with the family gathered around the bedside. Eventually, I made my apologies and left.

Returning home, I managed to get back to bed for a little while but, before very long, the alarm was calling me back to work, to a new day, and to Mass. As I put on the vestments for the Mass and tried to prepare myself for the celebration, I was overwhelmed with tiredness and exhaustion. Thankfully, the ritual of what needs to be done before Mass (including a short time of silent prayer) carried me through and before long I found myself ascending the altar steps. Very quickly, and almost miraculously, my energy returned, and I was ready for the offering of the Mass. Somehow, the Mass does that; it brings life and healing and strength, even when you least expect it.

When I'm celebrating Mass, I am struck again and again by the cosmological nature of what we are about. As Christians, we believe that the Mass is transformative and that, by the very celebration of the Mass, grace is effected—that the life, death and resurrection of Jesus is made repeatedly available for both the living and the dead, indeed for the whole world. The God who created the entire cosmos has given us through, with, and in Jesus Christ the gift of the Mass as a way of sanctifying and transfiguring

1. *CCC*, §1156.

everything that is: from the tiniest seed or insect to the far far away planets about which as yet we know nothing. God, who created all that is, seen and unseen, does not, I believe, withhold the transformative grace of the Mass from the totality and entirety of all creation. What could be a greater sign of that first love which motivates God to create, than to continually provide the means by which the whole of creation, known and unknown, human, animal, and plant, can be, in some mysterious way, a recipient of that continued grace and love?

So, the whole of the cosmos, including animals, is often to be found at the heart of the Mass: in Scripture, in song, in the prayers of the liturgy, in symbolism, and in praise of God.

In an ancient text of the Mass known as the Liturgy of Addai and Mari, which has been in continuous use by some of the Eastern Orthodox churches since the seventh century (but existing much earlier than that), we read, "Worthy of praise from every mouth and confession from every tongue and of worship and exaltation from every creature is the adorable and glorious name of thy glorious trinity."[2] We note that, from this ancient prayer, "every creature" is caught up in the worship and exaltation of the Almighty. In this venerable and historic text there is no question over whether animals share in the worship and praise of God, and that it is at the Mass that this reality is celebrated.

In the Egyptian Anaphora of Serapion (from about the fourth century), the worshipper joins in "Thanks to Thee Who hast made heaven and earth and all therein, the earth and all that is on the earth, the sea and rivers and all that is in them,"[3] undoubtedly including all of God's creation and gathering-up the animals in this act of praise. There is, it seems, excellent historical precedence for accepting that the eucharistic prayers of the church intend to include animals in their praise of God.

Also in the fourth century, the Apostolic Constitutions, a collection of historic liturgical books, contain examples of Mass as celebrated at that time in Greece: "May it be truly meet and right before all things to hymn thee who art indeed the living God, who art before the beginning of created things, of whom the whole family in heaven and earth is named . . . the giver of all good things, above all cause and origin, ever unchangeable and immutable, from whom as a source, all things came into being."[4] Echoing

---

2. Bouyer, *Eucharist*, 147.
3. Bouyer, *Eucharist*, 200.
4. Bouyer, *Eucharist*, 253.

the creation accounts in Genesis, this eucharistic prayer recognises that God is the creator of all things and that to acknowledge such is to worship him. There are many similar examples from the earliest liturgies of the church which testify to the place of animals in the plan of God for the earth and which, when named in prayer, add to the praise which is rightly God's; they are not overlooked or ignored or neglected; rather, they are seen for who they are: creatures of God, given to the world for a reason and, more than that, those who, because they share in the life of God and participate in the life of the world, join in the praise of the creator.

In the much-revered Liturgy of St. James (fourth century), we are invited to pray thus: "How truly meet and right . . . to praise you, to hymn you, to bless you, to adore you, to glorify you, to give you thanks! You, the creator of every creature, whether visible or invisible, the treasury of eternal good things, the source of life and immortality, the God and Master of all things, who are hymned by the heavens and the heavens of heavens, and all their powers, the sun and moon and the whole choir of stars, the earth, the sea and all that is found therein . . ."[5]

A popular hymn, "All Creatures of Our God and King," based on the "Canticle of the Creatures" by St. Francis of Assisi, sets the scene beautifully for an understanding of how the liturgy of the Mass, and other Christian liturgies, draws together all of creation in praise of God: "All creatures of our God and King, lift up your voice and with us sing: alleluia!" The final verse begins: "Let all things their creator bless."[6] St. Francis instinctively understood that each and every part of creation: sun, moon, stars, animals, plants, was called into being by God and that, through the redeeming power of Christ's death and resurrection, all could join in one universal song of eternal praise in glorifying God for such salvation.

St. Francis sees no need at all to deny animals this absolute right, since he wants to show clearly that in creation there is praise—that the very existence of something is an act of praise—that in an element of creation, any element, just being fully what it is created to be, God is praised. Animals, in being animals, exist to praise God! God has the right, we might say, that the whole of his creation (all the separate yet united parts) should be free to praise him who first created them. Volcanoes, mountains, bread, wine, women, men, children, apes, snakes, caterpillars, elephants, sheep, chickens, trees, grass, plants—all are created by God, in his eternally loving way,

---

5. Bouyer, *Eucharist*, 270.
6. *Laudate*, Hymn 694, by William Draper, ca. 1915.

and discover their real meaning in him who brought them into being. It is through praising him that we/they are enabled to become who we/they truly are.

The Mass also explores, often through the Scriptures, but also in the prayers of the liturgy, the symbolism of animals as part of God's creation. Animals can be used to show us things about God, about Jesus himself, and about ourselves.

In St. John's Gospel, John the Baptist points to Jesus and declares emphatically, "Behold, the Lamb of God" (John 1:29). The ancient people of Israel customarily slaughtered a lamb as an offering of repentance for sins committed (see, for example, Lev 4:32, where we learn that, twice a day, at the temple in Jerusalem, a lamb was slaughtered as a sin-offering). Historians tell us that, at the temple in Jerusalem, other sacrifices were offered too, such as peace offerings, fellowship offerings, votive offerings, offerings of consecration. In the book of Exodus, we are told that the lamb of sacrifice must be "without blemish" (Exod 12:5), and that the Passover lamb will be the definitive sign of the freedom from oppression and slavery of the people of Israel. Effectively, the sacrificial lamb becomes the absolute sign and symbol of liberation and joy (Exod 12:51). The prophet Isaiah also speaks of God's "suffering servant" who is oppressed and afflicted yet does not open his mouth; and who will be led like a lamb to the slaughter (Isa 53:7; See also Isa 52:13–53:12).

There are many images, especially from the Middle Ages, of Jesus depicted as a lamb. It is from the scriptural sources which I have mentioned (and others) that the artists are inspired. The connection between the innocent, pure lamb, meek and silent, and the crucifixion of Jesus, sinless and unspeaking, is clear. Using animals symbolically helps us to deepen our understanding and to grow in faith.

The ancient Israelites, who often lacked the economic means to offer a lamb as a sacrifice, were permitted to offer a dove, a creature of less economical value. A dove, which belongs to the pigeon family, is known to be an affectionate bird, both to its mates and to its offspring. In many cultures, in antiquity as well as in modern times, a dove is a symbol of peace. The correspondences between a dove and Jesus Christ are noteworthy; both spilled their blood when being offered up as sacrifices, and to both are attributed qualities of affection and peace. Jesus, additionally, is often referred to as the Prince of Peace (see Isa 9:6). St. John, in John 1:32, also describes, in terms of a dove, thus referencing this aspect of peace, the powerful presence of the Holy Spirit descending on Jesus, as recounted by John the Baptist.

All that having been said, we remember that, despite its unquestioned historic significance for the people of the time of Jesus and before, there is no actual biblical evidence to suggest that either Jesus or his disciples took part in the everyday common custom of sacrificing animals, even during their visits to the temple. The message of Jesus, commanding love of neighbour, and of forgiveness, not condemnation, implies that both he and his followers chose a different path. We know, for sure, that Jesus, as an observant Jew of his day, took part in the Passover meal, and it is in this context that he institutes the Eucharist—but there is no clear indication in the text of what he ate (Matt 26:20–29; Mark 14:17–25; Luke 22:14–20). We may assume that Jesus ate what all other Jews ate at Passover, but this cannot be absolutely confirmed from the Scriptures. Further, students of church history remind us that the early church, perhaps quite surprisingly (given that the sacrifice of animals was considered as foundational to Israel, and to Judaism's self-understanding at the time), completely rejects this part of its Jewish heritage and marks the way as noticeably divergent for followers of Jesus.

Animal sacrifice has no place in the life of the Christian—nor, indeed, has it ever. With the sacrifice of Jesus on the cross, temple worship comes to an end. The significance of the Last Supper/crucifixion taking place at Passover proclaims Jesus as the new Passover Lamb who offers his own body and blood in sacrifice. It is accomplished (*John 19:30*): the work which the Father gave Jesus to do is concluded—and that work? To reveal the Father (which the temple worship failed to do). Redemption is powerfully effected, and the empty sacrifices of the temple are now fully revealed as meaningless. Whilst the purpose of the death of Jesus is to show us this profound truth, and his self-offering on the cross is primarily about the redemption and salvation of the whole world, at the same time a beautiful corollary is that no more animals need to die in sacrifice. It is not necessary. A new order has begun. The One True Lamb has been sacrificed. The old order has passed away.[7]

Perhaps, then, the most important message in all of this is that Jesus, as the True Lamb who takes away the sins of the world, has given his life

---

7. See the film by Anderson and Waters, *Christspiracy*, which asks the controversial question, "How would Jesus kill an animal?"

once, only once, and once for all (see Rom 6:10) and thus liberates the need for any more lambs (or other animals) to be slaughtered.

Sometimes within the Bible, animals are used as messengers too: think about the serpent in the garden of Eden (Gen 3:1), or the efforts of Balaam's ass to show his human companion, despite Balaam's insistent cruelty to the creature, that the angel of the Lord is there before his very eyes (Num 22:32–33), if he would but look. In both examples, God even grants the animals the gift of human speech. The lengths to which God will go to show his people his care and concern for them, and the agency and the importance of the creatures which he uses to do so, is very apparent. Maybe animals are here because, without them, the full picture of creation is incomplete; because we humans need them on those occasions when we can't see for looking?

The prophet Job can help us. He says, "But ask the beasts and they will teach you; the birds of the heavens, and they will tell you; or the bushes of the earth, and they will teach you; and the fish of the sea will declare to you. Who among all these does not know that the hand of the Lord has done this? In his hand is the life of every living thing and the breath of all mankind" (Job 12:7–10). To Job it seems very obvious that animals instinctively have a perception of the mind and purposes of God which humans all too often fail to recognise.

Let's consider what happens to the bread and wine at Mass. Catholics (and many other Christians) believe that, by the power of the Holy Spirit, and through the grace of transubstantiation, the bread and wine become truly the body, blood, soul, and divinity of Jesus Christ. This fundamental teaching of the church is not just a nice idea, but a profoundly important understanding of the action of God in engaging with the world. The church's decisive and authoritative explanation about how the invisible substance (inner reality/essence) of the bread and wine truly, remarkably, and by God's grace, become the Body and Blood of the Lord is very much a jewel in our Catholic crown. God receives from us the ordinary and the everyday gifts of bread and wine (which we only have because he first gave them to us: wheat and grapes) and, because of his loving generous nature, God gives them back to us, invested with new and even greater meaning: the Body and Blood of Jesus.

The transformation of earthly gifts (given first by God) offered (back) to God through Christ, which are then returned to us as gifts with an even more precious reality, show us the power of God's desire to transform the whole world. God, after all, will stop at nothing to restore to fullness the whole of his creation, whatever it takes. The bread and the wine used at Mass, fruits of the harvest and so essential for human living, may be seen to represent the totality of all created things, and the way in which God transforms the ordinary into the holy and the extraordinary, including you and me.

Further, I suggest that if God can (and does) effect such profound transformation with simple fruit and grain on the one hand, and with human beings on the other, surely, he can do it too with the entirety of his animal creation. In transubstantiation, we see how the substance of the bread and wine becomes, at Mass, the Body and Blood of Jesus. It is, therefore, not difficult to believe that the same God who makes such a wonderful and beautiful thing happen at every celebration of every Mass throughout history and throughout the world, can and will also grant animals a share in the good things that he offers to all of the cosmos. As the hymn famously says, when referring to the glory of the real presence in Holy Communion, "for how can he deny me heaven, who here on earth himself hath given?"[8] The power of God to create and to recreate, to renew and to provide, is endless and inexhaustible—for all of his creation.

The heart of the Mass, following the high point of the Gospel reading, is the Eucharistic Prayer. It is this prayer which contains the words of Jesus from the Last Supper, and during which the moment of consecration takes place, and the bread and wine truly become the Body and Blood of Jesus. Each Eucharist Prayer begins with a preface, an important narrative outlining salvation history as intended by God for the whole world. The preface may be broad or specific, depending on which event in our Christian story is being celebrated. Some of these prefaces contain references which are helpful for answering the question that this chapter poses. For example, Common Preface III (for regular use on weekdays) says, "And so it is right that *all your creatures serve you*. . . . Therefore, we too, extol you with all the Angels."[9] Here the prayer acknowledges the right and freedom of all creatures—angelic, human, and animal—to serve and glorify God. This is the vocation of all created beings.

One of the Sunday prefaces rejoices in how God has "laid the *foundations of the world*" and has "arranged the changing of times and seasons," instinctively linking God's plan for all, human and animal, with his plan

---

8. *Laudate*, Hymn 662, by Alphonsus Ligouri (1696–1787), "O bread of heaven."

9. *Roman Missal*, Common Preface III, 648.

for every aspect of creation,[10] while another of the prefaces for Christmas acknowledges that God in Christ is "raising up all that was cast down, [that] he might *restore unity to all creation.*"[11] An Easter preface goes further: "For with the old order destroyed, a *universe cast down is renewed, and integrity of life is restored . . .*"[12]

During Lent, when we focus on the work of Christ in redeeming the world by his death and resurrection, we hear, "Since by the wondrous power of the Cross your judgment *on the world* is now revealed and the authority of Christ crucified." The Crucified One is he who restores all things to unity and ushers in the kingdom of heaven. This cosmic sense of the work of the cross surely includes all animate, sentient beings too. Common Preface I allows us to see this more clearly: "In him (Jesus) you have been pleased to *renew all things* . . . and by the blood of his Cross brought peace *to all creation.*"[13]

It seems that, embedded in the very core of the church's liturgy, which intentionally celebrates and proclaims the death and resurrection of Christ, there is an acknowledgement that the Christ-event *restores all things* by the power of the cross, and that all aspects of creation are, because of Jesus, being brought back to that fullness with God the Father for which they were first brought into being, and which we see in the peaceable kingdom of Genesis and Isaiah, and which is also prefigured in the heavenly banquet of the book of Revelation (19:11–13). Animals are part of this vision, and the God who created them surely does not exclude them.

The text of Eucharistic Prayer III following the Sanctus says it most clearly of all. There we read, "You are indeed Holy, O Lord, and *all you have created rightly gives you praise*, for through your Son our Lord Jesus Christ, by the power and working of the Holy Spirit, *you give life to all things and make them holy.*"[14] Not only are all things (including animals) created and enlivened by God, but they (like us) perhaps have within them the potential to point beyond themselves to the beauty of the One who created them.

St. Francis, echoing many of the beautiful psalms that we find in Scripture (see, for example Pss 148:10–13 and 150:6), speaks of all creatures existing to praise God, declaring that their very presence in the world tells

10. *Roman Missal*, Sundays in Ordinary Time, Preface V, 614; my emphasis.
11. *Roman Missal*, Preface for Christmas II, 574; my emphasis.
12. *Roman Missal*, Preface for Easter IV, 598; my emphasis.
13. *Roman Missal*, Common Preface I, 644; my emphasis.
14. *Roman Missal*, Eucharistic Prayer III, 684–88; my emphasis.

of the mighty work of the creator and how all creatures, human and non-human, find their destiny in the praise of God, and in living in communion with God.[15] Common Preface IV states that although God has "no need of our praise, yet our thanksgiving is itself your gift, since our praises add nothing to your greatness, but profit us for salvation." God doesn't need our praise but, when creation praises God, the elements of that creation are brought together in harmony and unity and thus fulfil their vocation. It is not God who is changed when we praise him, but those who are doing the praising: human and animal. The song of the lark, the howl of the wolf, the cry of the cheetah—all these are elements of non-human animals praising God and conforming, by their praise, to his perfect design and original plan.

Perhaps the preface which helps us most is that for the Solemnity of Jesus Christ, Universal King (observed the Sunday before Advent Sunday; the last Sunday of the liturgical year). There we read, "For you (Father) anointed your Only Begotten Son, our Lord Jesus Christ, with the oil of gladness as eternal Priest and King *of all creation*, so that, by offering himself on the altar of the Cross as a spotless sacrifice to bring us peace . . . he might present to the immensity of your majesty an eternal and universal kingdom, a kingdom of truth and life, a kingdom of holiness and grace, a kingdom of justice, love and peace."[16] I am readily persuaded that this kingdom of justice, love and peace, this eternal and universal kingdom, is not for humans only, and that God can consciously intend and desire that all of his creatures have a place in that kingdom of truth, love, and holiness. This idea is further suggested in one of the prefaces for holy martyrs, where we read, "Therefore, *all creatures of heaven and earth* sing a new song in adoration";[17] a sentiment echoed, word for word, in the proper preface for the Solemnity of the Most Holy Body and Blood of Christ (Corpus Christi).[18]

I am very aware, when I elevate the Host before Holy Communion and say, "Behold the Lamb of God. Behold him who takes away the sins of the world; blessed are those called to the supper of the Lamb," of the symbolism of the One who gave his life that we might live—the suffering, spotless Lamb. I am aware of the import of this part of the Mass and of the reverence which it is due. (At the same time, I'm acutely aware of

---

15. Francis of Assisi, "Canticle of the Creatures."
16. *Roman Missal*, Preface for Christ the King, 546; my emphasis.
17. *Roman Missal*, Preface II of Holy Martyrs, 638; my emphasis.
18. *Roman Missal*, Preface for Corpus Christi, 538.

the lambs and many other animals, throughout the world [including in the UK], whose lives are taken from them, but who have no voice or say in the matter. That particular moment at Mass is perhaps a good time to pray for them, and for an end to all forms of cruelty and violence to animals.)

Let us not forget, finally, that the Bible has all creatures themselves relying on God for their every need (like us) and thus praising and glorifying him, especially in the psalms. In Ps 104, we read, "O Lord, how manifest are your works! In wisdom you have made them all; the earth is full of your creatures. Here is the sea, great and wide, which teems with creatures innumerable, living things both small and great" (24–28).

Psalm 148 is more explicit: "Praise the Lord from the earth, you great sea creatures and all deeps.... Beasts and all livestock, creeping things and flying birds! ... Let them praise the name of the Lord, for his name alone is exalted" (7–11).

The Mass, being the supreme act of liturgical worship, brings humans and other animals together in uniting heaven and earth, so that the creator is glorified. The Mass thus unifies the entirety of heaven and earth in a supreme act of praise of God, and in sanctification of all things that exist.

From Laudato Si', Pope Francis

> It is in the Eucharist that all that has been created finds its greatest exaltation. Grace, which tends to manifest itself tangibly, found unsurpassable expression when God himself became man and gave himself as food for his creatures. The Lord, in the culmination of the mystery of the Incarnation, chose to reach our intimate depths through a fragment of matter. He comes not from above, but from within, he comes that we might find him in this world of ours. In the Eucharist, fullness is already achieved; it is the living centre of the universe, the overflowing core of love and of inexhaustible life. Joined to the incarnate Son, present in the Eucharist, the whole cosmos gives thanks to God. Indeed, the Eucharist is itself an act of cosmic love: "Yes, cosmic! Because even when it is celebrated on the humble altar of a country church, the Eucharist is always in some way celebrated on the altar of the world." The Eucharist joins heaven and earth; it embraces and penetrates all creation. The world which came forth from God's hands returns to him in blessed and undivided adoration: in the bread of the Eucharist, "creation is projected towards divinization, towards the holy wedding feast, towards unification with the Creator himself."

Thus, the Eucharist is also a source of light and motivation for our concerns for the environment, directing us to be stewards of all creation.[19]

Prayer

Father, we praise you with all your creatures.
They came forth from your all-powerful hand;
they are yours, filled with your presence and your tender love.
Praise be to you!
Son of God, Jesus,
through you all things were made.
You were formed in the womb of Mary our Mother,
you became part of this earth,
and you gazed upon this world with human eyes.
Today you are alive in every creature
in your risen glory.
Praise be to you!
Holy Spirit, by your light
you guide this world towards the Father's love
and accompany creation as it groans in travail.
You also dwell in our hearts
and you inspire us to do what is good.
Praise be to you! Amen.

(Part of *A Christian Prayer in Union with Creation* from *Laudato Si'*)[20]

---

19. Francis, *LS*, §236.
20. Francis, *LS*, §246.

8

How Does the Holy Spirit Help Us to Understand Animals?

*When Jesus was baptised, immediately he went up from the water,
and behold, the heavens were opened to him,
and he saw the Spirit of God descending like a dove and coming to rest
on him.*

(MATTHEW 3:16)

I REMEMBER, AS A music student, being very struck by a biblical reference in some of the literature of the Royal College of Music, where I had three very happy years: "the letter kills, but the Spirit gives life" (2 Cor 3:6). It seemed to me to be the perfect motto for what we were trying to do as musicians. The written notes on the manuscript paper are important, indeed there is no composition without the actual dots, but the music only comes to life when it is performed. A Beethoven or a Mozart symphony can look incredible on the page and be subject to all kinds of analysis and study by musicologists, but it is in listening to the music and hearing the work being played, that real excitement and revelation is found. There is, in a sense, a significant difference between what is written (black dots on a white page) and what is heard (sublime, potentially life-changing music).

How Does the Holy Spirit Help Us to Understand Animals?

The church teaches clearly that the Holy Spirit, proceeding from the Father and the Son (as we say in the Creed), brings life and grace.[1] The *Catechism of the Catholic Church* reminds us that the work of the Spirit and of Jesus Christ are one, and we read that "Christ's whole work is a joint mission of the Son and the Holy Spirit."[2] Essentially, the Holy Spirit is gift: bestowing, within God's good creation, freely given graces for the upbuilding of his kingdom on earth as it is in heaven. If we are to live an authentic Christian life, we need the help and power of the Holy Spirit. To be a Christian is to have received the Holy Spirit in baptism, in confirmation, and in the celebration of all the sacraments. Many of us, having been confirmed by the bishop, have heard the words, as he anoints us on the forehead, "be sealed with the Gift of the Holy Spirit."[3]

In chapter 1, we looked at the peaceable kingdom as outlined in Genesis (1–2), as foreseen in Isaiah (11), and envisioned as restored in Revelation (5). We recognised that in those passages (and others), animals have God-given life; that they exist because God has called them into being and that he loves them. In this sense, we can infer that animals become, by God's express desire, living souls (*nephesh chayam*). For the Christian, this can only be possible by the grace and power of the Holy Spirit—the ever-living, creative, regenerative, redemptive power of God himself. A living soul is a soul animated and graced by the Holy Spirit. It is reasonable to suggest that animals, like humans, may be enlivened by the power of the Holy Spirit, the Spirit who is always working jointly in union with Christ to transform and redeem the whole world.

Looking at the book of psalms in the Old Testament, we see that the Holy Spirit animates and inspires creaturely life, learning that when the Spirit is withdrawn, they die. In Ps 104, the writer declares before God that the earth "is full of your creatures" (v. 24):

> These all look to you, to give them their food in due season.
> When you give it to them, they gather it up;
> when you open your hand, they are filled with good things.
> When you hide your face, they are dismayed;
> when you take away their breath they die and return to their dust.
> When you send forth your Spirit, they are created, and you renew the face of the ground. (27–30)

---

1. *CCC*, §2017.
2. *CCC*, §727.
3. *Order of Confirmation*, Catholic Truth Society, 2016.

It is the Spirit who is the life-giver; the Spirit who animates and brings growth; the Spirit who is the heart and soul of what it means to be created by God; the Spirit in whose breath living things find vigour and essence. The psalmist calls us to see the truth of this, and seems to open up the possibility that animals, like humans, have potential-in-God, because they are Spirit-created (and breath-filled) in a mysterious and beautiful way.

St. Athanasius of Alexandria (297–373), known as Athanasius the Great and Athanasius the Confessor, a teacher of the faith and defender of the truth against heresy, wrote the following extraordinary words:

> [The Word, Jesus Christ] produces a single melody . . . and, holding the universe like a lyre, draws together the things in the air with those on earth, and those in the heaven with those in the air, and combines the whole with the parts, linking them with his command and will, and thus producing a single beauty and harmony, a single world and a single order within it . . . . [Jesus Christ] extends his power everywhere, illuminating all things visible and invisible, containing and enclosing them in himself, [giving] life and everything, everywhere, to each individually and to all together—creating an exquisite single euphonious harmony.[4]

Indeed, the Spirit who gives life to all creatures is the Spirit, working in a joint mission with the Son, who creates a harmony and a purpose for the whole of creation, human, animal, and plant. The whole of creation is thus Spirit-inspired, Spirit-led, and finds its eternal destiny in Jesus by the work of the Holy Spirit.

St. Athanasius also writes that, "The Spirit of the Lord fills the universe. Thus, King David sings, 'Where shall I go from your Spirit?' (Psalm 139:7). Again, in the Book of Wisdom, it is written, 'For your immortal spirit is in all things' (Wisdom 12:1). If the Spirit fills all things, the Word (Jesus) is present in all things."[5] As if to make a point, he also affirms, "When the Word visited the holy Virgin Mary, the Spirit came to her with him, and the Word in the Spirit moulded the body and conformed it to himself, desiring to join and present all creation to the Father through himself, and in it to reconcile all things, having made peace, whether things on heaven or things upon the earth."[6]

---

4. Athanasius, *Contra*, 41, cited in Linzey and Regan, *Compassion*, 8.
5. Athanasius, *Letter to Serapion*, 72.
6. Athanasius, *Incarnation*, cited in Linzey and Regan, *Compassion*, 81.

For St. Athanasius, it appears that the Holy Spirit is given to the whole of the created order, filling the complete universe and leading that same universe to find its identity and truth in Jesus.

Remaining with the Old Testament, the prophet Joel can perhaps help. The seer confidently declares a prophecy from the Lord: "I will pour out my Spirit on all flesh" (2:28). Note that the translation is clear; it is on all flesh that the Spirit is poured. There is no distinction here between animal or human flesh but all flesh, the flesh of which Isaiah also prophesies when he declares, "The glory of the Lord shall be revealed, and all flesh shall see it together" (Isa 40:5). It is all flesh which shall both receive an outpouring of the Spirit and, by virtue of having received that Spirit, live in the wonder and dynamism of the glory and power of the Lord.

To even the harshest sceptic around this matter, and considering the intent of the biblical writers, we might simply ask the question, "Can there be flesh that is not Spirit-filled?" It is reasonable, having looked at the scriptural message, to answer this question in the negative; the writers of the passages are clear: God gives his Spirit to all whom he wills, all flesh throughout the fullness of the earth. If, in recognising the gift of the Spirit in our own lives, we have a God-initiated desire to honour and value the Spirit in the lives of those around us then, for me, this could include animals too. It is interesting to note that St. Peter, as recorded in Acts 2:16, during his sermon on Pentecost day, repeats this passage of Joel (Acts 2:16–21, especially v. 17) and roots his experience of the Holy Spirit, and his call to his hearers to receive the Holy Spirit, in this understanding. For Peter, too, the Holy Spirit is given to all flesh, and the Holy Spirit transforms and changes the lives of all living beings.

We need to return again, albeit in passing, to St. Thomas Aquinas. In the Catholic tradition, there has always been a definite sense that there are different kinds of souls (at which we looked earlier) and that only humans have supernatural souls because their souls, unlike anything in animals, are rational and supernatural, and therefore immortal. However, we can see here, *pace* St. Thomas, that a huge question is raised: What is the basis of any soul or spirit, but that given by the Holy Spirit? If not from the Holy Spirit, then from where might such a spirit or soul come? What else could we understand by soul or spirit? All spirituality and interior life find its origin and purpose in the third person of the Holy Trinity: the Holy Spirit. Perhaps, in trust and faith, it may be acceptable to assign to all of God's creatures such graces as, it seems to me, they probably already have.

Animals in Heaven?

We can now look at the beautiful, yet somewhat mysterious passage in Romans 8, where St. Paul writes about life in the Spirit. Towards the middle of the chapter, he reminds his readers that "if the Spirit of him who raised Jesus from the dead dwells in you, he who raised Christ Jesus from the dead will give life to your mortal bodies through his Spirit who dwells in you" (10–11). For me, one implication could be: all flesh will experience in some mysterious way, the power of the resurrection. "Mortal bodies," says St. Paul, will receive life through the power of the Holy Spirit, even after death when, like in Jesus, the Spirit will be the agent of resurrection. Paul, though, wants to say much more than this. He speaks of a future glory for which he believes all those who are Spirit-filled are called and destined: "I consider that the sufferings of this present time are not worth comparing with the glory that is to be revealed to us. Creation waits with eager longing for the revealing of the sons of God" (18–19). The sons of God, God's children, those whom God has created, are presumably all those united through, with, and in Jesus; "they are sons in the Son": those filled with the Holy Spirit (thus, certainly human and probably animal), those who, with the aid of the Holy Spirit, work together to proclaim the gospel to all creation, each according to their own unique capacity.[7]

The "sufferings of this present time" are clear to see, even today, but there is hope for all, since suffering is not the end of the story. Paul goes further, telling us that "creation itself will be set free from its bondage to corruption and obtain the freedom of the glory of the children of God. For we know that the whole creation has been groaning together in pains of childbirth until now" (20–23). Sin and death, says Paul, are reminders that the end is still to come, and that the whole of creation (including the possibility of Spirit-filled animals) is groaning and in pain because we have a God-given sense that, whilst the effects of sin must be endured, we are destined for something greater, the glory that is to be revealed: eternity with God in heaven, achieved through the saving work of Jesus. "If we hope for what we do not see," says Paul, "we wait for it with patience" (25).

We still wait for all humanity, all animal-kind, all creation, to be redeemed and caught-up in the transforming power of the resurrection and ascension of Jesus. It is on this that our whole faith is based. Whilst the Christ-event (the death and resurrection of Jesus) is already accomplished, there is also a real sense of both the *now* and the *not yet* of the eternity for which we are destined. There are powerful glimpses of the "now-ness" of

---

7. John Paul II, *General Audience*, Rome, September 27, 2000

the kingdom, especially when we celebrate the sacraments, which allow us to experience, in those beautiful grace-filled moments, the reality of a heaven which is made present on earth—but, still, the fullness of that kingdom is yet to be realised, as we know, only too well, from our own experience.

St. Paul appeals to a Spirit-filled operation of hope in which all creatures in travail (you, me, animals) will be redeemed, and it is in this hope that we are saved. This reality is brought about by the power and action of the Holy Spirit. How could it be otherwise? There really would be no point in creatures finding the freedom of the children of God if they are not, indeed, the very offspring and delight of him who created them? Why would God want to redeem empty vessels or automata? For, says St. Paul, "In all things, we are more than conquerors through him who loved us. I am sure that neither death nor life, nor angels nor rulers, not things present nor things to come, nor powers, nor height, nor depth, nor anything else in all creation, will be able to separate us from the love of God in Christ Jesus our Lord. I am speaking the truth in Christ. . . . My conscience bears me witness in the Holy Spirit." (8:37–9:1).

St. Cyril of Jerusalem echoes St. Paul when he says, "The Holy Spirit is supremely Great Power, divine and unsearchable, living and rational. And it belongs to him to sanctify all things that were made by God through Christ."[8] The Holy Spirit is, by the power of God the Father, the sanctifier of all life, human and animal.

These matters are important in our understanding of who animals are, why God created them, and how they are potentially sanctified with the power of the Holy Spirit. It has to be said that, generally, the role of the Holy Spirit in engendering and inspiring all creaturely life within God's creation has been somewhat eclipsed in the Catholic and wider Christian tradition (except, of course, in human beings). It is to the Holy Trinity that we must turn: God is creator, of human and animal; God, in Christ, is redeemer, of the entirety of his creation; God is sanctifier and advocate, of human and animal.

In the Holy Spirit, we are recipients of so many gifts (1 Cor 12:1–11), with these gifts bearing much fruit (Gal 5:22–23), each according to need and benefit. There are, of course, many more, perhaps indiscernible, gifts and fruits of the Holy Spirit. It is possible, I suggest, that it's not only humans that possess such graces from God, but so, too, may animals.

---

8. Torrance, *Theology*, 225.

Pope John Paul II said in 1990 at a public audience that "animals have a breath of life, received from God. Under this aspect, man, having come forth from the hands of God, appears in solidarity with all living beings. . . . 'When you send forth your Spirit, they are created, and you renew the face of the earth' (Psalm 104:30). The existence of creatures thus depends upon the action of the breath-spirit of God, which not only creates, but even conserves and continually renews the face of the earth."[9]

Even if we conclude that animals are not Spirit-filled in the same way that humans are, the fact that humans have this divine capacity to receive the Holy Spirit, and are beautifully enlivened by that same Holy Spirit, suggests that our care and concern for animals must be all the more generous, all the more benevolent, reasonable, and unselfish.

The Catholic poet and Jesuit, Gerard Manley Hopkins (1844–1889), powerfully speaks of the Holy Spirit interacting and sustaining every part of God's creation:

> And for all this, nature is never spent;
> There lives the dearest freshness deep down things; . . .
> Because the Holy Ghost over the bent
> World broods with warm breast and with ah! bright wings.[10]

At the Royal College of Music, we literally breathed new life into the dots on the page which, for many, are largely illegible and nonsensical scribblings made up of crotchets and quavers. Instead, by the power of performance, we had the privilege and the grace of revivifying and resurrecting the composer's original dream. It is the Spirit which gives life: to music, to you, to me, to animals, to all in God's great creation. The Spirit gives life. Indeed, as we say in the Creed, the Holy Spirit is the Lord and Giver of Life—for all beings.

Laudato Si', Pope Francis

> I would like from the outset to show how faith convictions can offer Christians, and some other believers as well, ample motivation to care for nature and for the most vulnerable of their brothers and sisters. If the simple fact of being human moves people to care for the environment of which they are a part, Christians in their turn

---

9. John Paul II, "Udienza Generale," §4.
10. Hopkins, *Poems and Prose*, cited in Linzey and Regan, *Compassion*, 13.

"realize that their responsibility within creation, and their duty towards nature and the Creator, are an essential part of their faith." It is good for humanity and the world at large when we believers better recognize the ecological commitments which stem from our convictions.[11]

Prayer

What is a charitable heart? It is a heart which is burning with charity for the whole of creation, for men and women, for the birds, for the beasts—for all creatures. He who has such a heart cannot see or call to mind a creature without his eyes becoming filled with tears by reason of the immense compassion which seizes his heart; a heart which is softened and can no longer bear to see or learn from others of any suffering, even the smallest pain, being inflicted upon a creature. This is why such a person never ceases to pray also for the animals . . . that they may be preserved and purified. That person will pray even for the reptiles, moved by the infinite pity which reigns in the hearts of those who are becoming united to God. Father, give me and all the world a heart such as this, [through Jesus Christ our Lord]. Amen.

(St. Isaac of Nineveh, ca. 613–ca. 700, slightly adapted)[12]

---

11. Francis, *LS*, §64, quoting Pope John Paul II, message for World Day of Peace, 1990.

12. Catholic Concern for Animals, "Prayers," §13.

9

What Can the Catechism Tell Us about Animals?

*God created the great sea creatures
and every living creature that moves,
with which the waters swarm, according to their kinds,
and every winged bird according to its kind.
And God saw that it was good.*

(GENESIS 1:21)

I STOOD NERVOUSLY OUTSIDE the large superstore. Being a potential source of conflict to others does not sit at all comfortably with me. I had already distributed to the group gathered with me the placards which read, "Stop FrankenChickens." Pictured on those boards were young chickens who had been pumped full of growth hormones to ensure faster-than-natural development. In fact, the chickens in these situations (billions of them in the UK) grow so quickly that, very soon in their young lives, they can no longer stand and end up covered in sores and filth—and all this before their short existence is ended in slaughter at just thirty-five days. The pictures are hard to see, and the suffering is very evident. The natural life span of a healthy chicken is up to seven years. Compelled to speak up for the chickens who are exploited like this every year, I had called together, via social media, a small band of like-minded friends who, with me, either stood in silence or gently offered information leaflets to shoppers as they came and went. The superstore had been told of our little vigil and were kind and respectful to us. This was not an occasion for me to dress visibly as a priest, but I was in my parish and many folk, including Catholics, recognised me. It is discomforting to be seen by others in these situations, especially as such activity can be thought subversive but, in fact, those who knew me thanked me for my witness, took a leaflet, and promised to consider their own choices. One or two of the passing shoppers were not at all happy with our gentle protest but, generally, people were polite and willing to discuss the matters which we were hoping to raise. It's a bit like the call to preach the good news of Jesus: "How are they to hear without someone preaching?" (Rom 10:15). I and my friends were not there, specifically, to preach or, indeed, to judge. We all realised that people must be free to make their own decisions. But we wanted, for the sake of those poor suffering chickens, to provide some context to assist them in that decision-making process. Maybe only one person would change the habits of a lifetime that day, but that would save countless chickens throughout the life of that individual. And the chickens really do suffer so much . . .

The vision of the catechism, in terms of what it means to be created by God and to live in the world, is both beautiful and challenging. The catechism seeks to express everything that Catholics believe, and it tries to answer the questions that Christians may have about life, the universe, and everything else besides. The current version of the catechism, promulgated by Pope St. John Paul II in 1992, is a work of wisdom and power and, of course, has a high degree of authority as an official teaching document of the church.

Animals are briefly mentioned in the catechism where, as we saw in chapter 2, four paragraphs are given over to the subject under the title "Respect for the Integrity of Creation": sections 2415 to 2418. Back in the thirteenth century, St. Thomas Aquinas had said two things: that "it is not wrong for man to make use of animals by killing them, or in any other way"[1] and that "charity does not extend to irrational creatures."[2]

In the last few decades, scholars of all Christian denominations have begun to question the views of Aquinas. Many theologians, reflecting on the sense in which understanding grows and develops gradually over time and through the power of the Holy Spirit, would now propose a different perspective, and have been willing to develop and build on this thinking.

---

1. Aquinas, *Summa Theologiae*, II, Q64, A1.
2. Aquinas, *Summa Theologiae*, II, Q25, A3.

We could even say that the catechism now stands within a new, developing tradition (and, further, that *Laudato Si'* certainly does). In paragraph 2416, the catechism states clearly that "animals are God's creatures" and that "humans owe them kindness," seeming to refute what had been stated by St. Thomas.

The same paragraph tells us that animals have their own dignity in and of themselves, a dignity not dependant on humans, and which is integral to their identity, because it is God-given. This idea challenges the received impression that animals are only valuable inasmuch as they are useful to human beings: "By their mere existence [animals] bless God and give him glory."[3]

The catechism also reminds us that human beings have a moral obligation in respect of animals and in the care of creation, stating that animals and the rest of the created world "cannot be divorced from respect for moral imperatives," calling us, at the same time, to have a "religious respect for the integrity of creation."[4]

The catechism does allow for the use of animals for food and clothing, work and leisure, and for medical and scientific experimentation—but always within "reasonable limits" and only within a context of "contributing to caring for or saving human life."[5] It seems that when we do use animals in this way, if we choose so to do, it must always be within strict parameters and in a spirit of alleviating unnecessary suffering in these creatures, ensuring that the animals are treated with dignity. It would be interesting to unpack what, exactly, the term "reasonable limits" means in this context. It appears to be an open-ended and unresolvable statement, since each of us may well draw the line in a different place. It would be helpful if the catechism had been clearer on this matter.

Finally, in section 2418, we are reminded, as we've already seen, that it is beneath the human condition to intentionally harm an animal (for fun, or for sport, or for other forms of entertainment, we might say): "It is contrary to human dignity to cause animals to suffer or die needlessly" and that "one can love animals."[6]

---

3. *CCC*, §2416.
4. *CCC*, §2415.
5. *CCC*, §2417.
6. *CCC*, §2418.

What Can the Catechism Tell Us about Animals?

The catechism, unsurprisingly, upholds the obvious traditional Catholic and biblical view that human beings are the crown of God's creation,[7] and affirms that this truth runs through every aspect of the church's understanding of why and how God created the world. It is in this context that, because of the human vocation to dominion and stewardship, promoted by both the Bible and by the catechism, humans are required to treat animals well. Further, choosing to try and see everything through the lens of Jesus Christ's compassion and saving work (which is, after all, one of the key purposes of the catechism—to help us live a Christ-like life), it is equally important that Christians, individually and corporately, be invited to challenge their own understanding of how they relate to animals. Is there anything that we do (consciously or otherwise), as believing faithful Christians, that could be contrary to our own dignity as a human being, because of the ways that we treat animals—even by implication? John Berkman, in "Prophetically Pro-Life: John Paul II's Gospel of Life and Evangelical Concern for Animals," suggests "that God has chosen humanity to be an image of God's own rule in the world" and that, therefore, surely, this dominion which is given to humans is to be exercised as God exercises his all-powerful dominion: with creativity, generosity, love, and compassion.[8]

The catechism attempts to help us make sense of our faith and to join up all the dots. The Catholic faith is, naturally, beautifully comprehensive. Looking at the catechism, we see that each of its many teachings relates intrinsically to all the others and that, for a full understanding of our faith, we need to see our Catholic Christianity in its entirety. It makes no sense to isolate or to select only some parts of what the church teaches. We remember that received authority is a *unity*, and all the more powerful for it. At the same time, the church, in her wisdom, respects our freedom and our ability to intellectually form our consciences, and asks us to make choices accordingly. We could say, for example that, according to the catechism, the church does allow for animals to be killed so that we can eat meat or wear leather, so long as those animals are killed humanely and with dignity.[9] As followers of Jesus, the One who lays down his own life, rather than taking the lives of others, that perhaps raises particular moral challenges for us.

Revisiting section 2418 of the catechism, the whole matter of the choices which we make is brought into clearer focus. There may have

---

7. *CCC*, §2417.
8. Berkman, "Prophetically Pro-Life," 57n40.
9. *CCC*, §2417–18.

been a time when humans *needed* to eat animals and to wear their skins as clothing. Today, there may still be some places in the world where that is necessary. However, we could also conclude that it is *not necessary* for us, in twenty-first century Britain, to eat animals and that, because it is so easy to make other choices, we do not need to be a party to the unnecessary suffering that goes with seeing animals as food or clothing. Indeed, perhaps we could consider consciously choosing to avoid doing so. It is, of course, possible to eat a perfectly healthy and nutritious diet without causing animals to suffer and to die needlessly. Legally permitted, so-called humane slaughtering of animals still causes what many would objectively agree is immense fear, pain, and great suffering for the animals concerned. The supermarkets where we customarily shop have shelves groaning with plant-based food options, all offering delicious and healthy alternatives to meat and dairy. It is possibly more consonant with our faith for us to choose not to eat meat or to wear leather, and so on, and thus avoid, as much as possible, even any unintentional suffering for the animals involved.

The choices which any of us make, informed by the teachings of the church, are what enable us to grow in faith and to place Christ at the centre of our lives. Neither the church, nor the law of the land, forbids the slaughter of animals for food. By the same token, because we *can* eat meat and wear animal skins, does not mean that we *must*. Those who choose not to do these things are no less practising Catholic Christians for making such a choice and, by so doing, may be offering a small personal contribution towards recreating the peaceable kingdom, on earth as it is in heaven. Additionally, factory farming and its related activities would seem to many, to be a very long way from the ways in which animals were bred, housed, and slaughtered at the time of Jesus. It is legitimate, perhaps, to ask the question as to whether Jesus would bless the current practices and customs in animal agriculture which are so prevalent throughout the world.

I'm going to mention Pepe again. I remember one day sitting down to a plate of roast beef and having Pepe on my lap at the table. I caught sight of him, so happily snuggled up, and as content as ever just to be with me. As I tucked into the food in front of me, I reflected (yet again) on how much Pepe meant to me, knowing so well that I couldn't bear to see him suffer in any way. Early on in his little life he had needed major surgery on two occasions, and I learned, as I entrusted him to the veterinary hospital, how seeing him suffer (and not being able to solve the problem of his suffering) had made me suffer immensely too. Then I saw the beef on my plate.

What about the cow who had died for me so that I could choose to eat this meat? Had she suffered too? Perhaps throughout her life on a factory farm, she had never really known the happiness and contentment which Pepe so readily and so evidently enjoyed. What about the very end of her life? She will have been transported from the factory farm to the slaughterhouse. What must that have been like? Would she and her fellow cows have had a sense of what was happening? Did they intuit the end for which they were destined? I actually can't bear to think what it must have been like to arrive at that slaughterhouse with all of its smells and loud noises and violence. Yet, here I was, seemingly happy to eat the meat before me. It suddenly struck me very forcibly: what is the real difference between Pepe and that cow? Both want to live and to be happy, after all. I believe, as a Christian, that both are created by God; both have a degree of autonomy and an awareness of their surroundings and deserve, as beings who are God-created, to share in God's goodness as much as any other. The clash of logic hit me. The cow has as much right to live as the dog on my lap. It sounds odd but, in that moment, I made a similar emotional connection to the cow on my plate as I had made with Pepe from day one.

Why tell this story? Well, we can follow the *Catechism of the Catholic Church* freely and faithfully, without needing to be persuaded that a different lifestyle, to which we may be ethically drawn, and where there is noticeably less suffering for animals, is available to us; a lifestyle that is still, of course, accordingly Christian and Catholic. From that day, which I remember so vividly, to this, I freely made the choice, there and then, and again and again, not to consume meat or dairy products anymore. It was/is, of course, a decision completely in harmony with Catholic teaching.

In looking at *Laudato Si'*, we notice that the formal thinking of the church around this and similar areas continues to develop; that the tradition of the church is not static and unmoving but can be understood within an appropriate cultural and historical context. Pope Francis teaches us, in this encyclical, that we have been given creation as our home; that there is a profound interconnectedness of environmental, social, economic and human issues. In this sense, *Laudato Si'* builds on previous teachings, highlighting the responsibility of humanity to care for the earth, whilst also advocating for an integral ecology that considers both human and environmental well-being.

The Second Vatican Council, and much church teaching before, says very little (if at all) about ecological concerns or about matters relating to the place of creation in the life of the Christian. *Laudato Si'* begins to redress that apparent imbalance and puts creation (all of it) firmly on the Catholic agenda, stressing the importance of sustainability and other ethical considerations in economic practices. It is an astonishing reversal of the church's sensitivity to such huge matters and is something of a positive win for animals. Because of this input from the Holy Father, the place of creation in the life of the Christian and of the Catholic Church must now remain central. This is an exciting and very seriously important development in Catholic thinking, to which I will return later. For now, it is enough to say that *Laudato Si'* is a natural and organic development of the church's revered teaching tradition, building, as it does, on the work of the Catechism of the Catholic Church.

St. Anselm of Canterbury (1033–1109), doctor of the church and Archbishop of Canterbury, is said to have been moved to feelings of compassion for animals. It is recorded that he wept for them, for example, when he saw them caught in the hunter's net. Despite hunting being such an acceptable custom for his day (even as it is today), he was horrified at the cruelty shown to such innocent creatures. One story tells how a hare was being chased by hunters and dogs through the forest, all of whom were keen to catch and kill the animal. Anselm stopped his horse and allowed the hare to rest under the horse's protective body, while the laughing men around restrained the dogs, for fear of upsetting the good bishop. Anselm scolded the men and challenged them to consider for a moment the fear that the hare must be experiencing, before moving on and forbidding the dogs from attacking the poor creature.[10] As a man who spent much of his life preaching and teaching the doctrines of our faith, Anselm seems to have intuitively understood that it flies in the face of human dignity to cause unnecessary suffering to animals. This great bishop of the church had a remarkable intellect but, more importantly, seemed to understand the nature of God as compassion and generosity to all creatures.

I remember an occasion when I was walking my dogs. Georgie loves to forage and to hunt in the undergrowth. While all Pepe needs to be happy is a ball to chase, Georgie is more complex. On one occasion, as he searched for prey in the hedgerow at a local park, Georgie caught in his mouth a tiny baby wild rabbit. I was horrified and demanded that he immediately release the little one. By that time, other dog walkers had gathered around and were watching the spectacle of Georgie not wanting to free the rabbit and

---

10. See Eadmer, *Life of St. Anselm*, for this and other similar stories

me demanding that he should; it was quite a battle of wills. "Don't worry," said one of the locals, as he heard my demanding cries, "there are plenty more rabbits where that one came from." I was immediately saddened by such a pragmatic and cold response, which reduced that rabbit to a plaything and a commodity. The rabbit, like Georgie, deserved to live and to be free from harm. The wild is the wild, fair enough, but here I had a chance to make a difference for that rabbit and wanted to do so. I can only pray that God will be as kind in dealing with me. The rabbit was actually unharmed and, at my heightened insistence, Georgie let the creature go and all was well that ended well.

From Laudato Si', Pope Francis

> It follows that our indifference or cruelty towards fellow creatures of this world sooner or later affects the treatment we mete out to other human beings. We have only one heart, and the same wretchedness which leads us to mistreat an animal will not be long in showing itself in our relationships with other people.[11]

Prayer

Triune Lord, wondrous community of infinite love,
teach us to contemplate you
in the beauty of the universe,
for all things speak of you.
Awaken our praise and thankfulness
for every being that you have made.
Give us the grace to feel profoundly joined
to everything that is.
God of love, show us our place in this world
as channels of your love
for all the creatures of this earth,
for not one of them is forgotten in your sight.
Enlighten those who possess power and money
that they may avoid the sin of indifference,
that they may love the common good, advance the weak,

---

11. Francis, *LS*, §92.

and care for this world in which we live.
The poor and the earth are crying out.
O Lord, seize us with your power and light,
help us to protect all life,
to prepare for a better future,
for the coming of your Kingdom
of justice, peace, love and beauty.
Praise be to you!
Amen.

(Part of *A Christian Prayer in Union with Creation* from *Laudato Si'*)[12]

---

12. Francis, *LS*, §246.

10

Is It Appropriate to Pray for Animals and to Bless Them?

*Sing to the Lord with thanksgiving;
make melody to our God on the lyre!
He covers the heavens with clouds; he prepares rain for the earth;
he makes grass grow on the hills.
He gives to the beasts their food, and to the young ravens that cry.*

(PSALM 147:7–9)

I RECALL, SOME YEARS ago, being appointed to a new parish as assistant priest. I knew the parish priest very well, since I had worked with him previously. I was genuinely delighted at having the opportunity to be assisting him in parish ministry once again. He had taught me so much by his own modest example of what, for an individual priest, an authentic life of pastoral care really looks like. When he was growing up, his mother had suffered from a long and debilitating illness. He never forgot how faithfully and diligently his own parish priest had called to visit his mother every week without fail, bringing her Holy Communion and praying with her. He suggested that it was this experience of undeniable commitment that had fostered his own thoughts of a vocation to the priesthood.

So far, so good. However, I was very worried about the priest I was due to replace. You see, Fr. Daniel was everything that I wasn't: he'd had a glittering career in academia and had already achieved a physics PhD, even though he was still so young; he was an outstanding musician who could turn even the most uninspiring composition into a magical piece of art; he could preach effectively to young and old alike, and leave the hearer spellbound by his marvellous homilies; he was popular, likeable, friendly, amusing, and a natural pastor. I could not see any of those things in myself and I became very anxious about having to follow him. "How can I possibly follow Fr. Daniel?" I said to the parish priest. "I simply cannot compete." The wise parish priest didn't scold me for my self-centredness or for my obvious lack of faith in God's will for me (he was far too kind for that). Instead, he said something I will never forget. "Terry, Fr. Daniel is indeed all the things that you mention, and so much more—but remember, none of those things will get him into heaven. If you want to live your priesthood faithfully and to God's glory (and, by implication, go to heaven), become a man of prayer and from there all other things will flow." It hit me like a brick: it's not meant to be about me; it's meant to be about God, and about allowing God to work in me and with me and through me, in the name of Jesus Christ, aided by the powerful force of the Holy Spirit. How had I been so foolish and self-regarding? It was a moment of revelation, but also a time to grow up and to become a man: a time to put away childish things (such as what other people think of me). As if to back up that revelation, he later said to me, "Terry, 5 percent of the parishioners will love you, 5 percent will dislike you (perhaps intensely), but 90 percent just want to come to Mass." I often remember the power of such words when I'm tempted to think that priestly ministry is about me, rather than about Jesus.

I have been trying to pray seriously for over forty years and I am still very much a beginner—barely off the starting blocks, really. I completely see the value of prayer and I strive, daily, to make quality time for prayer. We know from the gospels that Jesus spent long periods in prayer and often escaped from the busyness of daily life to be alone with his Father. Anyone who has been on a retreat will know the value of stepping away for some quiet time to pray, to be alone with the Lord, and to be recreated in stillness and silence.

In my amateur way, I am learning more and more that prayer is, in fact, about what I *don't* say, and instead, is concerned with giving generous time to the Lord, allowing him the space to speak into my heart. Of course,

Is It Appropriate to Pray for Animals and to Bless Them?

God can and does use any daily event or happening to communicate his will to me, but giving him a scheduled time every day, where I can listen with the ears of my heart (as per the prologue in the *Rule of Saint Benedict*) and actually hear what he is saying, is truly life changing. It takes the pressure off too. Prayer becomes about listening and waiting, rather than about speaking and doing. Patience is required, and a dogged determination not to find something better with which to occupy myself. In the end, if we humbly try to persevere with prayer, we become aware of our greater need of God and how genuinely dependant we are on him for all that truly matters. I can't recommend it highly enough.

These times of quiet communion with the Lord where I can be still and listen, have only deepened my awareness of animals as part of God's glorious creation. I can no longer take them for granted and imagine that they are here for my use, any more than I can spread wings and fly through the air. My experience of drawing closer to the Lord and having a sense of him drawing closer to me in prayer has, if you like, finely tuned my awareness of creation, and shown me that animals matter—that they are here for a reason, that they give glory to God by their lives, that they can help me to grow in faith. If this is not a matter for my prayer, then I don't know what is.

Earlier, we looked specifically at the prayer of the Mass, noting that liturgical prayer has a distinctive pattern and characteristic. Much liturgical prayer is made up of intercession and of bringing to God specific intentions. We must ask, because our need is so great. Liturgical prayer is also full of the praise of God, and of thanksgiving for his saving work in Jesus Christ. Together, the People of God reach out to him in joyful praise, for the great gift of salvation.

Personal prayer, complementing, as it does, liturgical prayer, can have a unique and intimate quality, and we will want to bring to it our own particular concerns and thoughts. God, of course, hears our prayer, both liturgical and personal. Our prayer makes a difference. We know that it's perfectly normal to pray, for example, for good weather. The weather is not a person, obviously, nor a conscious, animate being, and yet we think nothing of imploring the heavens for a good dose of sunshine for some important event, or for a successful year of harvest. We bless cars and houses and so much else. In particular, we bless animals too.

We know that animals can feel and think and experience life. We only have to look around us to see that. We delight at the birds singing in the park, or at the pigs running across the field to greet us when we bring food, or at the chimpanzees careering through the trees at high-speed playing and interacting with one another. These are the actions of sentient beings; creatures brought into existence by God for a purpose. They are not insignificant; they are those on whom the planet relies for a healthy ecosystem and with whom humans are called to live in harmony. We not only can, but must, pray for the animals with whom we coexist. They are here for a reason. They need our prayers. It would surely be the most natural thing in the world to pray for our family cat if she was suffering, or for the wounded fox we see limping away in the back garden. Our natural sympathy and empathy kicks in and we want to do the best that we can, even in our somewhat limited circumstances, for these animals. For the Christian, prayer is a natural response to any event. We bring these creatures in need from our heads to our hearts and into our prayer and offer them to God with whatever necessary plea we need to make. To consciously choose to draw these creatures into the ambit God's redeeming love, even if we see no immediate fruit from such a prayer, is to commune with the creator and to enter into a profound experience of unity both with God and with the creature(s) for whom we are praying.

In the Jewish tradition, blessing is understood a little differently from the way in which we have come to understand it as Christians. For Jews, to bless something or someone is to thank and praise God for that thing or person. If we think about the prayers of the offertory at the Mass, we are reminded of the moment where the priest says, "Blessed are you, Lord, God of all creation for through your goodness we have this bread to offer." This ancient Jewish format for prayer, familiar to Jesus, is known as the *berakah* prayer. At this point in the Mass, the priest is praising God for the gifts that God has given us and, if you will, blessing (thanking) God for all the good things with which he continually showers us.

For Christians, building on this ancient Jewish tradition (like so much of our prayer and liturgy), and wanting always to thank and praise God for his goodness to us, blessing has come to be experienced as a prayer that God will set apart and make holy some particular object or person for a special purpose (the blessing of wedding rings, for example). The Jewish elements of thanksgiving and praise are still implicit in this Christian act of blessing, for there is a recognition that everything ultimately comes from, and returns to God, but there is a more nuanced sense of wanting God to do something specific for the thing or person being blessed. It is a decisive moment after which there is seen to be some kind of new spiritual investment in the person or object being blessed.

It is, therefore, very natural for Christians to want to bless animals. To be sure, if we can bless cars and houses and crops, then we can certainly bless animals, many of whom, after all, have blood and flesh and bones like us, and share the world with us in a very real way. In blessing these creatures, we see God's hand at work in sanctifying those whom he has given to us for the good of the planet and, equally, for the good of the human race. It is the most natural thing in the world for us to want to give praise and thanks to God for animals and, at the same time, to ask him to set them apart with his blessing, for his greater glory.

Many parishes and cathedrals, around the feast of St. Francis of Assisi (4th October each year), hold animal blessing services and liturgies. These times of prayer and praise are quite a sight to behold and are as beautiful as they are chaotic. But there is no difficulty here. This is what God does through his church: blesses that which he has already given to us so that it becomes invested with new, and deeper, meaning. Christians will naturally turn to God to do this for the animals which they bring to him in this way. It is, quite simply, second nature.

As animal blessing liturgies reveal, having animals at Mass or at some other gathering for prayer comes with its challenges. Anyone who has sought to improve the liturgy of Palm Sunday with the inclusion of a donkey will know this for sure. However, I have tried to say, through the ideas that we've been sharing, that animals have a valued and God-given place in the world; that they are not second-class citizens; that they cannot speak for themselves in a way that is understandable to humans, so we must be their voices; that they not only share the planet with us but can reveal to us (if we would but see) the depths and the purposes of a loving God. This being the case, they have a place in the church (and, for some people, within the church building too) as much as anyone else. Wisdom and common sense must prevail, of course but, within reason, it would even seem appropriate to bring companion animals with us to Mass.

In Matt 19:14, Jesus says, "Let the little children come to me, and do not hinder them, for to such belongs the kingdom of heaven." It is a radical and surprising thing to hear. So often, children are marginalised and, we are told, are to be seen and not heard. Jesus challenges the accepted culture of his day, where children were usually seen as property, and demands that we see them with new eyes. The gospels, of course, are full of examples of Jesus behaving in this way. Maybe, in many ways, animals are not unlike children.

Animals, too, especially in today's companion animal culture, are frequently seen and treated as property (we talk of dog *owners*, for example). Free-roaming animals are viewed from a distance to be tolerated, so long as they don't invade *our* space. I remember seeing, somewhere online, an image of a woman who is preparing a chicken for the family lunch. She has one hand in the cavity of the fowl, as she stuffs the carcass in readiness for the oven. At the very same time, she turns and screams at her cat for bringing in a captured bird from the garden. In exasperation, she cries out something like, "How dare you do such a disgusting thing to that bird in my house!" Her cognitive dissonance is plain to see: she, in fact, continues to do disgusting things to a dead bird in her kitchen—the very thing for which she scolds the cat (and she, not the cat, is the one who is dignified with the gift of reason). Further, if she knew the conditions in which that chicken she is preparing had been living on a factory farm, she might reconsider her words. We fail to make the important connections about who animals are and why they are important, and instead see them as for our use (eating the chicken, for example, in the cartoon) or to be despised (condemning the cat for bringing in the captured bird, who appears to have little or no value).

Animals cannot speak for themselves. To our ears, they have no evidently recognisable voice or language, just like young children. It is, however, possible for us to be aware when animals (and tiny children) are suffering or when they are happy, even though they cannot specifically tell us; we can intelligently and emotionally deduce it. We can choose, in a context of prayer, to start to notice animals in a new way and, in the spirit of the gospel, to truly *see* them for who they are. When Jesus challenges the culture of the day by turning the commonly accepted view of children on its head, he makes us think again. As humans, we may reasonably conclude that we tend towards an element of cultural bias—of not having truly *regarded* animals for so long and in so many situations, for perhaps simply accepting that animals are here for our use and for our convenience, to be disposed of when we've finished with them. But they have no voice. They have no power. They have no means of objecting. They need us, in the name of Jesus, to be their voice, their power, their advocates.

So, we should certainly pray for animals—God knows, they (and so many others) need it in today's prevailing culture of death; we can certainly bless them, for their lives are often ignored or made inexpressibly difficult by humans. Like children, they have so little. We, on the other hand, have so much. I suggest that, in fact, we owe it to God, and to the animals themselves, to let them come, and to notice them for who they truly are. Andrew Linzey puts it characteristically succinctly when he says that "animals cannot represent their own interests. Individuals who cannot adequately represent themselves have to depend upon benign moral representation. This consideration marks animals, along with vulnerable human subjects, notably infants, and young children, as a special case. There are, therefore, strong grounds for extending to these beings, special consideration."[1]

St. Isaac of Nineveh (died ca. 700), saw every reason to pray for animals (as we have seen[2]), declaring that a genuinely loving heart is one which is "burning with charity for the whole of creation, for men, for the birds, for the beasts . . . for all creatures. . . . That is why such a man never ceases to pray also for the animals . . . . He will pray . . . moved by the infinite pity which reigns in the hearts of those who are becoming united to God."[3]

A liturgical prayer book of the Catholic Church, the *Rituale Romanum*, provides excellent examples of how normative it has been for centuries in the church to bless animals and to call down God's grace upon them. The ritual provides appropriate Bible readings and suitable litanies for such an occasion. A modern American version has a helpful passage drawn from Scripture, with words for the priest to say, where we read, "The animals of God's creation inhabit the skies, the earth, and the sea. They share in the fortunes of human existence and have a part in human life. God, who confers his gifts on all living things, has often used the service of animals or made them symbolic reminders of the gifts of salvation. Animals were saved from the flood and afterwards made a part of the covenant with Noah (*Genesis 9:9–10*). The paschal lamb calls to mind the Passover sacrifice and the deliverance from the bondage of Egypt of the people of God (*Exodus 12:13–14*); a giant fish saved Jonah (*Jonah 2:1–11*); ravens brought bread to Elijah (*1 Kings 17:6*); animals were included in the repentance enjoined on humans (*Jonah 3:7*). Animals share, too, in Christ's redemption of all God's creation. We therefore invoke divine blessing upon these animals and, as we do, praise the Creator."[4]

---

1. Linzey, *Animal Suffering*, 35.
2. See the prayer concluding chapter 8.
3. Lossky, *Mystical Theology*, 111.
4. *Roman Ritual*, 410, §949.

In the *Rituale*, there are blessings for cattle, herds, and flocks, as well as for horses and other animals. We also see blessings for sick animals and for fowl and birds of all kinds. Rather wonderfully, there are blessings for bees and for silkworms too. Following the blessing prayer, the ritual suggests that the animals may be sprinkled with holy water. The blessing of animals is clearly, and has been historically, a rich tradition in the church and certainly has a valid place in our spiritual lives as Catholics.

Laudato Si', Pope Francis

> Ongoing research should also give us a better understanding of how different creatures relate to one another in making up the larger units which today we term "ecosystems." We take these systems into account not only to determine how best to use them, but also because they have an intrinsic value independent of their usefulness. Each organism, as a creature of God, is good and admirable in itself; the same is true of the harmonious ensemble of organisms existing in a defined space and functioning as a system.[5]

Prayer

O Lord, how manifold are your works!
    In wisdom you have made them all;
    the earth is full of your creatures.
Here is the sea, great and wide,
    which teems with creatures innumerable,
living things both small and great.
They all look to you
    to give them their food in due season.
When you give it to them, they gather it up;
    when you open your hand,
    they are filled with good things.
When you send forth your Spirit, they are created,
    and you renew the face of the ground.
May the glory of the Lord endure for ever;
    May the Lord rejoice in his works!

5. Francis, *LS*, §140.

To the Father, in the power of the Holy Spirit, be all glory, through Jesus Christ our Lord. Amen.

(Derived from Psalm 104:24–25, 27–28, 30–31)

11

Why Does God Allow Animals to Suffer?

> *He was despised and rejected by men,*
> *a man of sorrows and acquainted with grief;*
> *as one from whom men hide their faces,*
> *he was despised and we esteemed him not. . . .*
> *All we like sheep have gone astray; we have turned*
> *—every one—to his own way;*
> *and the Lord has laid on him the iniquity of us all.*
> *He was oppressed, and he was afflicted, yet he opened not his mouth;*
> *like a lamb to the slaughter, and like a sheep*
> *that before its shearers is silent.*
>
> (ISAIAH 53:3, 6–7)

I WANT TO TELL you a little bit about Georgie, my Greek-rescue Brittany spaniel cross. Georgie is a heart-stealer and as handsome and adorable as it's possible for a dog to be. People often comment, when we are out and about on our walks, at what a good-looking dog he is. I agree—but I am more than a little biased.

Georgie came to me as a puppy from the streets of Greece. He had been born homeless and he and his brother were rescued by an animal charity and taken to a shelter. Probably he would have been quite young when he was rescued and so, hopefully, would have been spared a lot of the neglect and cruelty that stray dogs in so many countries experience. But it's impossible to know for sure.

Georgie is generally goofy, crazy, loving, and enjoys playing (especially tug-of-war). However, he becomes easily unsettled by loud noises, bangs, and busy, overpopulated environments. He cannot bear fireworks, for example, and all the noise and chaos associated with them. When he experiences a loud, restless situation he becomes immediately withdrawn, visibly anxious (manifested in shaking and whining quietly with his tail between his legs), and very noticeably afraid. To see him in this way is extremely upsetting. All those around him want to get close to him, to comfort him, and to end his evident unease as quicky as possible.

At these moments, Georgie's suffering is very real. As far as I am aware, he is not physically in pain (which is often how we tend to define suffering), but his experience of anxiety, fear, and immense disquiet, is obvious for all to see; he truly suffers. I find it best to sit with him, embrace him, and cover him with a tightly fitting blanket, while we wait for the time to pass. Eventually, he will come round but, in that moment, it is clearly distressing for him (and for those around him).

Sadly, animal suffering (like human suffering) is everywhere. I want to avoid a litany of examples of how very real animal suffering is. Suffice to say that, as we know so well, intentional cruelty exists, neglect and rejection exist, human arrogance and control over animals exists and, every day, millions of animals die unthinkable deaths in slaughterhouses in this country and throughout the world (after all, it is impossible, isn't it, to do an unkind thing kindly). Animal suffering is everywhere, even though it is very often consciously hidden from view. The philosopher Jeremy Bentham (1748–1832), when speaking of animals, raises the rhetorical thought that "the question is not, Can they *reason?* nor, Can they *talk?* but rather, Can they *suffer?*"[1]

Why do animals suffer? If we accept that a loving, benevolent God has created them, and that we are called, as human beings, to have wise dominion of the whole earth, why does that suffering exist?

The answer, of course, is that it's a part of the tragedy of the fall. We learn in Genesis 3 that the peaceable kingdom is fundamentally disrupted when the humans in the garden choose to turn their backs on God and, instead, to make themselves into gods. In the narrative, God is clear that the

---

1. Bentham, *Introduction*, 157.

humans may eat of the fruit of the trees in the garden, but that they should not even touch the tree of the knowledge of good and evil. The man has been created by God from the dust of the earth and the woman, his perfect companion, is created from his rib; thus man and woman together share a fundamental unity. For all that, and as like to God as they are, complete power over good and evil is reserved only for God. Having eaten of the forbidden fruit from the tree, meant only for God, the humans, by their own actions, experience an autonomy and a self-reliance for which they are not originally created. Because of their desire for power, they have alienated themselves from God and God, in his goodness and mercy, ever indulgent to his creation, honours that desire, allowing them the freedom to choose to separate themselves from him. However, with choices come responsibilities, and the humans must now live with the consequences of their actions. The *Catechism of the Catholic Church* says that "the account of the fall in Genesis 3 uses figurative language, but affirms a primal event, a deed that took place at the beginning of history. . . . [The] whole of human history is marked by the original fault freely committed by our first parents."[2] By these acts, human beings are unable to live the happy life in the peaceable kingdom for which they were originally created; the breaking of the divine commandment (not to eat from the tree), therefore destroys the contentment for which they/we were created, ruptures our harmony with God, and destroys our unity with all of creation. The fruit of sin, as St. Paul says in his Letter to the Romans (6:21), is ultimately death but, because of the corruption caused by the free choice of the humans to ignore God's command, suffering exists as a kind of foretaste of death.

When speaking about sin, Julian of Norwich says that during one of her visions, "Our Lord reminded me in a general way of all the things that are not good, and of the shame, contempt, and utter humiliation he suffered for us in his life and death. And of the pain and suffering of all the creatures he has made, physical and spiritual."[3] She suggests that both humans and animals and, maybe, even inanimate parts of God's creation, suffer with Christ on the cross because of human sin. Despite the fact that animals do not consciously sin (because they cannot reason in the way that humans reason), still they suffer, as Christ suffered, owing to the problem of evil caused by the fall.

2. *CCC*, §390.
3. Julian of Norwich, *Revelations*, 38.

These matters affect us all. Each of us recognises the challenges involved in trying to live Christlike lives, and of our own tendencies to choose darkness over light, to put ourselves first, and to be distracted from holiness by the "sights that dazzle" and the "tempting sounds we hear."[4]

Because of their disobedience (freely chosen), the humans in the story experience distance and alienation both from God and from creation. Thus, the rupture which is created is applicable to humans, to animals, and to all created things. Nothing can be the same again because of the choices of those first humans, who were originally commanded to "till and keep" the planet (Gen 2:15), not to exploit it for their own ends (which is exactly what they do when they choose disobedience and eat the fruit of the tree of the knowledge of good and evil). Suffering and death thus become the lot of all living things, especially for humans and for sentient beings like animals.

Regrettably, much of the suffering of animals is caused by humans who could be said to (at least sometimes) display a general attitude of dominance over them. Hopefully, some of our previous thoughts have challenged that bias assumed by humans towards animals, and we can begin to see these divinely created beings in a new light. Their suffering is real. Perhaps there are ways in which we can make changes in our own lives and, instead, reach out to these very often defenceless and ignored creatures.

Andrew Linzey makes the important point that it is when we make the "moral discovery that animals matter in themselves, that they have value in themselves, and that their suffering is as important to them as ours is to us,"[5] that we begin to see just how much animal suffering should concern us. As Christians, surely, we cannot be blind to, or disregarding of, such suffering. Linzey goes further: "In [factory] farming, we keep animals captive, and make them subservient to our purposes; we frustrate their basic behavioural needs; and we kill them in a frequently inhumane way, which makes them liable to suffering. We do all this, even though they have not harmed us, and even though they do not pose any threat to our life or well-being. They cannot 'assent' to their maltreatment or even vocalise their own interests. Theirs is a state of moral innocence and blamelessness; they are without means of defence and are wholly vulnerable. In short, we have made them entirely dependent upon us; they deserve, as a matter of justice, special moral solicitude."[6]

---

4. *Laudate*, Hymn 875, "O Jesus I Have Promised," Bode, 1869.
5. Linzey, *Animal Suffering*, 56.
6. Linzey, *Animal Suffering*, 103–4.

The *Compendium of the Catechism of the Catholic Church* (2005), in a chapter reflecting on the commandment to love our neighbour as we love ourselves, reminds us that "people must treat animals with kindness as creatures of God."[7] The church recognises that animals do suffer, and that their suffering probably contravenes the commandment to show them neighbourly love, even when that suffering is supposedly authorised or considered acceptable by humans.

St. John Henry Newman (1801–1890), a Victorian convert to Catholicism from Anglicanism, was an intellectual tour de force and an expert in matters of theology, philosophy, education, and prayer. On one occasion, while preaching a sermon in Oxford, he equated the suffering of animals to that of the suffering of Jesus on the cross. He makes a powerful point: can all suffering, he asks, human and animal, find its meaning through the death of Jesus? Preaching from Isaiah 53:7 (a passage concerning the suffering servant—usually understood as prophetically pointing to the coming of the Messiah), and which refers to a "lamb that is led to slaughter," Newman states that because Scripture itself compares Christ to this "inoffensive and unprotected animal," so we, in turn, can be free "without presumption or irreverence, to take that image as a means of conveying to our minds those feelings which our Lord's suffering should excite within us."[8]

Newman goes on to ask the question, "For what was this, but the very cruelty inflicted on our Lord?" An extraordinary connection to make, and one which we can take very seriously, coming, as it does, from one of the church's greatest thinkers. The cruelty inflicted on Jesus Christ in his suffering and death is not unlike, Newman says, the cruelty still inflicted on animals. He concludes, "Think, then, of your feelings at cruelty practised on brute animals, and you will gain one feeling which the history of Christ's Cross and Passion ought to excite within you."[9] For Newman, the suffering of innocent animals at the hands of humans resonates deeply with the suffering of Jesus on the cross: the elements are all there: innocence, the lack of a voice, weakness, imprisonment, an imbalance of power and control, and so on.

Later, Newman makes an astonishing appeal for kindness to animals: "Now what is it that moves our very heart, and sickens us so much at cruelty shown to poor brutes? I suppose this: first, that they have done us no harm;

---

7. CCCC, §507.
8. Newman, *Parochial and Plain*, 2:133.
9. Newman, *Parochial and Plain*, 2:133.

next, that they have no power whatever to resistance; it is the cowardice and tyranny of which they are the victims which make their suffering so especially touching. . . . There is something so very dreadful, so Satanic in tormenting those who have never harmed us, and who cannot defend themselves, but who are utterly in our power."[10]

St. John Henry Newman eventually joined the Congregation of the Oratory, a community of brothers, founded by St. Philip Neri. Neri, as we saw, was himself an advocate for animals and it is unsurprising that Newman shared (and even develops) the views of his revered founder.

It was a joy for me, September 19, 2010, to be in Birmingham for the visit of Pope Benedict XVI and to witness, at a huge celebration of Mass with the pope, the beatification of John Henry Newman. His canonisation followed in 2019, at which the Prince of Wales (now King Charles III), represented the UK delegation; such was the importance of this historic event.

Laudato Si', Pope Francis

> We are always capable of going out of ourselves towards the other. Unless we do this, other creatures will not be recognized for their true worth; we are unconcerned about caring for things for the sake of others; we fail to set limits on ourselves in order to avoid the suffering of others or the deterioration of our surroundings. Disinterested concern for others, and the rejection of every form of self-centeredness and self-absorption, are essential if we truly wish to care for our brothers and sisters and for the natural environment. These attitudes also attune us to the moral imperative of assessing the impact of our every action and personal decision on the world around us.[11]

Prayer

O God, who has made all the earth
and every creature that dwells therein:
help us, we pray, to treat with compassion
the living creatures entrusted to our care;

---

10. Newman, *Parochial and Plain*, 2:133.
11. Francis, *LS*, §208.

Animals in Heaven?

that they may not suffer from our neglect
nor become the victims of any cruelty;
and grant that in caring for them
we may find a deeper understanding
of your love for all creation;
through Jesus Christ our Lord. Amen.

(Unknown)[12]

---

12. "Prayers and Liturgies," §2.

12

Why Did St. Francis Preach to the Birds?

> *How lovely is your dwelling place, O Lord of hosts!*
> *My soul longs, yes, faints for the courts of the Lord; my heart*
> *and my flesh sing for joy to the living God.*
> *Even the sparrow finds a home, and the swallow a nest for herself,*
> *where she may lay her young, at your altars,*
> *O Lord of hosts, my King and my God.*
>
> (PSALM 84:1–3)

JUST OUTSIDE THE EAST Sussex town where I grew up there was a huge factory owned by Buxted Chickens. This enormously successful company employed many locals, including members of my own family. The business was set up in about 1955 and quickly became a massive profit-making concern. The founder and managing director of the company had been a Battle of Britain pilot and then a London stockbroker, before consciously introducing American-style factory farming to the little Sussex village of Buxted: as far as I know, one of the first in the UK. As well as changing the diet of British families, he became fantastically rich. Starting out in a disused cow shed, the entrepreneur later introduced four environmentally controlled chicken sheds, capable of housing one hundred thousand birds each. Every shed was given its own farm manager and assistant manager to ensure effective oversight of the production line.

In a short time, three more sheds were added. At first, the company was interested only in rearing, plucking and chilling the chickens produced there, but with massive success and growth for the business, came the production of twenty-five thousand birds a week which had been reared, slaughtered, plucked, eviscerated, frozen and packaged—all on the Buxted site. By 1964, five hundred thousand chickens a week were being processed through the company's sheds, and people all over Britain were consuming chicken in ways of which were previously unheard, with the cheaper, more-readily available product that the business was bringing to market. By this time, the owner was probably the biggest chicken farmer in Britain (and perhaps Europe) and an immensely wealthy man, creating, as he did, a kind of revolution in British eating habits, making chicken the favoured meat of the table for millions.[1]

Buxted Chickens featured highly in my childhood because it was so much a part of the local scene. One could not walk past the factory and the chicken sheds without being repulsed by the stench of effluent and what I suppose must have been dying chickens. Likewise, an endless array of trucks, carrying chickens crammed into small crates, brought birds from other places to Buxted to be slaughtered and, in so doing, constantly clogged up the local roads. Every time one of these lorries passed by the locals would cover their noses in horror. This is a very visceral memory. I recall the foul smells, the sadness I naturally felt at seeing the trucks, and the dying, gasping birds forced into tiny portable containers. I also remember distinctly the shock I felt at how normalised this seemed to be. At that stage, I had not really discovered a voice of my own and, like everyone else, just kept quiet about it all, assuming that it was me who had the problem.

Recently, I saw a truck full of sheep very obviously being taken to the slaughterhouse. Some of them seemed lame and sick and, again, were crammed into the vehicle, whilst being expected to endure both a long journey and the immense heat of the summer's day. Without thinking, I did what Catholics do when we come across death: I made the sign of the cross. It was a natural, instinctive response to the fatal journey which these poor sheep were being forced to make. They had no voice, no say in their future, no means to object. They were seen as a money-making product and, although no one would generally choose to make them suffer, their lives were to be ended soon and so, well, who cares? They looked terrified. And I felt helpless. Making the sign of the cross was a natural response

1. See buxtedparishcouncil.gov.uk.

to their impending slaughter—but it won't have helped them to be spared their grim fate, or to be seen as creatures who have value in their own right; creatures who want to live, just like you and me.

St. Francis of Assisi seems to have understood animals. His love for creation and for animals is legendary and even our present pope, breaking with tradition and history, took the name of *Il Povero* (the poor one) from Assisi as a sign of his desire to seek out the poor and to care for the planet, the common home of all God's creatures. As Deborah M. Jones says, "Francis views animals as part of creation as a whole, where everything created is, in a real sense, sacramental. For him, everything that exists, since it comes from the heart of God, is a sign of the holy, a sacrament of the Divine. . . . Francis is the first exponent of 'theos-rights', or the movement for the 'democracy of all creatures', where every creature in creation is given its fundamental rights since it possesses those rights because it is a beloved creation of God."[2]

Francisco Bernadone of Assisi (1181–1226) was a rich young man with a huge inheritance coming his way, until he turned his back on all of that, following a deeply mystical and spiritual encounter with Christ on the cross. Following this life-changing experience, Francisco decided that he would devote his life to the poor by fully and authentically embracing poverty himself. Pietro Bernadone, Francisco's father, astounded at what he saw as his son's youthful, immature exuberance and recklessness, rebuked Francisco and ordered him to go and speak to the local bishop—no doubt with a firm hope that, with such authoritative intervention, Francisco might finally see some sense. But to no avail. Realising quickly that his son's mind was completely made up, and that there was no persuading him to reconsider (even by the bishop), Pietro declared Francisco no son of his, disowning him there and then. Francisco replied immediately, claiming that this surely didn't really matter, since his real father was his Father in heaven. In a flash, it became strikingly clear to Francisco that, if his biological father had disowned him, then even the clothes on his back were not his to keep. Right there, in front of the bishop and the people gathered in the town square, Francisco removed all of his garments and stood naked before them all—his potential embarrassment saved only by the bishop, who cast his cloak over him. Francisco quickly declared to all that he would now live his life only for God. It must have been quite a sight for the people of

---

2. Jones, *Compassion*, 68.

Assisi, seeing this popular young man dedicating his life to Christ in such a startling and self-deprecating way.

On hearing at Mass the passage from St. Matthew's Gospel that says, "Proclaim as you go, saying, 'The kingdom of heaven is at hand.' Heal the sick, raise the dead, cleanse lepers, cast out demons. You received without paying; give without pay. Acquire no gold or silver or copper for your belts, no bag for your journey, or two tunics or sandals or a staff, for the labourer deserves his food. And whatever town or village you enter, find out who is worthy in it and stay there until you depart" (Matt 10:7–11), Francisco was moved to vow publicly (according to his biographer Thomas of Celano): "This is what I wish; this is what I am seeking. This is what I want to do from the bottom of my heart."[3] His extraordinary life has been much documented, and he is one of the most beloved of the saints. Of him, St. Bonaventure (1221–1274) memorably said: "In things of beauty, he contemplated the One who is supremely beautiful, and led by the footprints he found in creatures, he followed the Beloved everywhere."[4]

In a famous story, depicted in art throughout the centuries, St. Francis is said to have preached to the birds. It is a huge part of the Christian tradition, as we have seen, to recognise the familiarity and the concern that so many holy women and men, through the ages, have had with animals. To these saints, animals are natural God-given companions and teachers, and help them to live out the Christian vocation of putting Jesus at the centre of all things. Why might St. Francis have preached to the birds? What does it tell us about him, about animals, and about ourselves?

Thomas of Celano further tells the reader how St. Francis often urged the civil authorities in his area to be ever mindful of gospel truths, encouraging them to look after the needs and welfare of all the local villagers, as well as being mindful to care for the animals and the birds. He had a heart, in the name of Jesus (and after his example), for all who are poor and vulnerable, human or animal. He even strongly recommended that the local councillors enact laws for the feeding of animals on Christmas Day. Francis "wanted the poor and hungry to be filled by the rich, and oxen and asses to be spoiled with extra feed and hay. 'If ever I speak with the emperor,' he would say, 'I will beg him to issue a general decree that all who can, should throw wheat and grain along the roads, so that on the day of such

---

3. Thomas of Celano, *First Life of St. Francis*, 22.
4. *Legenda Major, IX*, quoted by John Paul II, *Letter to Artists*, §22.

a great solemnity the birds may have an abundance, especially our sisters the larks."[5] Christmas, of course, celebrates the immense generosity of God who, out of extraordinary love for the world, becomes flesh in the womb of the Virgin Mary. St. Francis, who started the tradition of having nativity cribs as aids to devotion at Christmas saw, in the Child in the manger, vulnerability and benevolence combined. For him, it was unimaginable that Christmas could be celebrated without the generosity and goodness of God being extended to all those in particular need, including the animals. I can't help thinking that St. Francis would find the modern custom of enthusiastically feasting on animals at Christmas and Easter, and in all times of great Christian celebration, as an ironic and sad dereliction of this reality. Most people do not deliberately intend to cause suffering to animals, but sometimes, by unwarily observing tradition or custom, we can find ourselves accidentally, as it were, party to such cruelty. "Where is the generosity offered to others when innocent lives are consciously, and inhumanely, and unnecessarily ended, to celebrate that very generosity?" St. Francis might ask. It is an ethical question for us all.

Clearly, as is well-documented, Francis had an affinity with all of God's creatures and saw the human-animal relationship as a unity. He had an innate sense of how all creatures, by their very existence, honour and glorify God; that their lives are evidence of the need for us to find our true selves in the praising of God; that they show us, by their humility and utter dependence on God, how to praise God; that the marvellous things that they do and are (cheetahs running at high speed, tortoises living very long lives, bats using sound technology that would confound humans, and so on) are evidence of God's goodness and of our/their need to praise him for that goodness; that we and they are beautifully and wondrously interconnected.

St. Francis seems to have fundamentally understood that he/we and animals have a shared origin, that we are flesh and blood together, and that we are created out of love by God; that we exist because God has willed that we should; that God has a dream in his heart for each of his precious creatures, animal and human. Perhaps Francis could see in them what he saw in himself—his true identity as experienced in Jesus Christ.

In a stunning passage directly related to human vocations, but which is noticeably inclusive of "every creature," the church invites all living beings to consider this vocation to holiness, and to understand that their very existence can only find meaning in God through, with, and in Jesus Christ,

5. Fortini, *Francis of Assisi*, 531–33.

as St. Francis did: "Just as holiness is for all the baptised in Christ, so there exists a specific vocation for every living person; and just as the first is rooted in Baptism, so is the second connected to the simple fact of existing. The vocation is the providential thought of the Creator for *each creature*, it is his idea-plan, like a dream found in God's heart, because the creature is found in his heart.... Vocation is the divine invitation to self-realisation according to this image and is unique-singular-unrepeatable precisely because this image is inexhaustible.... *Every creature* expresses and is called to express a particular aspect of the thought of God. There he finds his name and his identity; he affirms and ensures his freedom and originality."[6]

St. Francis models this vocation perfectly, of course, but evidently sees the wider scope of all creatures having been created by God who has a "dream in his heart" for each; a remarkable thought and one which encourages us, with St. Francis, to see the reality of God in every living being.

For St. Francis, animals are not merely incidental, or happen to exist by accident but, rather, are meant to be here, have a right to be here, and should be treated accordingly. He baulked at all forms of cruelty or unkindness to animals and instead saw them as tender brothers and sisters deserving of our love.

It's also important to recognise that the love which Francis had for animals is a natural and organic extension of the love which he had for God: his desire to love and to care for God's creatures, is an instinctive result of his love for the God who created him and them. St. Francis saw the presence and image of God imprinted on all things[7] and used that inner awareness as a means of drawing closer to God.

By preaching to the birds, St. Francis demonstrates his deep reverence for all creatures and his desire to share the message of God's love and goodness with the entirety of creation. It is claimed that Francis said, "Preach the gospel; use words if you have to," although it is hard to find accurate attribution for this. Either way, this could have been a message which he, in his way, communicated to the birds. The birds don't speak words as we understand words, but instead, encouraged by the saint of Assisi, they could use well their tuneful voices to praise God in a new (and perhaps more beautiful) way.

For St. Francis, the birds can share, with us, in telling the story of Jesus in their perfect birdlike way, since God is the foundation of all creation,

---

6. Pontifical Work for Ecclesiastical Vocations, *New Vocations*, §13.a; my emphasis.
7. See Pius XI, *Rite Expiatis*.

and all creation needs to hear the message of the gospel. He preached the good news to the birds in the only way he knew and invited them (and you and me) to do the same. "Go into the world," says the gospel writer, "and proclaim the gospel to the whole creation" (Mark 16:15).

It is believed, though difficult to positively confirm, that the following exhortation to the birds is from St. Francis himself: "O Little Brother, that brims with full heart, and having nothing, possesses all, surely you do well to sing! For you have life without labour, and beauty without burden, and riches without care. When you awake, lo it is dawn; and when you come to sleep, it is eve. And when your two wings lie folded about your heart, lo there is rest. Therefore, having this great wealth, that when you sing, you give your riches to all." Amen to that!

St. Francis is among those saints who are specifically mentioned in the catechism as examples to emulate and to follow, appearing, in fact, in the short section concerning animals.

Buxted Chickens is now no more. The animal agriculture industry, however, has grown and grown, and continues to grow exponentially. More people are eating more meat than ever before. Taking the example of St. Francis, and looking into our animal-loving hearts, what might we consider adapting in our own lives, to honour and respect all the animals who suffer so terribly?

Laudato Si, Pope Francis

> But human beings are not completely autonomous. Our freedom fades when it is handed over to the blind forces of the unconscious, of immediate needs, of self-interest, and of violence. In this sense, we stand naked and exposed in the face of our ever-increasing power, lacking the wherewithal to control it. We have certain superficial mechanisms, but we cannot claim to have a sound ethics, a culture and spirituality genuinely capable of setting limits and teaching clear-minded self-restraint.[8]

Prayer

Lord God,

---

8. Francis, *LS*, §105.

no flash of beauty,
no enchantment of goodness,
no element of force,
but finds in you the ultimate refinement and consummation itself.
Eternal Father, who,
through Jesus Christ, our ascended Lord,
ever send your Holy Spirit to be the bond of fellowship in the Church:
unify in Christ, we pray, the whole created order;
who lives and reigns with you and the Holy Spirit,
God for ever and ever. Amen.

(Pierre Teilhard de Chardin)[9]

---

9. Chardin, *Hymn*, 138.

13

What about the Popes?

God said, "Behold, I establish my covenant with you and your offspring after you, and with every living creature that is with you, the birds, the livestock, and every beast of the earth with you, as many as came out of the ark; it is for every beast of the earth."

(Genesis 9:9–10)

Nineteen ninety-eight was the year that I hugged the pope. Very early one May morning, the six deacons from the Venerable English College in Rome made their way to the Apostolic Palace within the walls of the Vatican. We had been invited to share in the pope's early Mass. It was a fantastic privilege to have received such an invitation and there was an air of anticipation and awe as we navigated, with help of the Vatican Guard, the stairs and lifts within the various buildings. We went through enormous, high-ceilinged room after enormous room, and eventually approached the private chapel of the Holy Father. Although it was still very early in the morning, it was absolutely clear that Pope John Paul II had been there for a long while. He was so steeped in prayer that he seemed unaware of our arrival. Amidst hushed tones, we took our places on the chairs available, before I was suddenly whisked away by a Vatican official. I was duly asked to assist at the Mass and to stand at the side of the pope throughout, as his deacon. What an incredible honour.

It was an intimate Mass with only about twenty people present (mostly clergy and nuns), and I had a tangible sense of history as I became increasingly aware of the proximity of the pope. Here was the successor of St. Peter celebrating Mass, and I had the blessed opportunity of assisting him. It was an awesome and moving moment. At the Sign of Peace, I did a bad thing. I decided to hug the pope! I mean, why wouldn't I? I was never going to be this close to the supreme pontiff again. He seemed a little alarmed, but Mass proceeded in the usual way and no harm was done. Afterwards, there was an opportunity for photographs, and we were presented with a rosary by the Holy Father, who spoke a little English with us. As we were leaving, a Vatican official approached me and, wagging his finger, said kindly and with a smile, "We do not hug the pope." By then it was too late. The deed was done. I can now claim to have hugged not just the pope, but a saint of the church. The role of the papacy, and the history and authority that it represents, are key to a Catholic understand of the church, and plenty of popes have supported the view that animals matter to God, and so can matter to us too.

We have already seen that, for centuries, the commonly perceived teaching of the Catholic Church around animals is that these creatures can be viewed as machines with no real moral value, and that they can often be understood only in terms of their usefulness to humans. The dominion argument, derived from Genesis 2, which we've previously considered, naturally reflects the understanding that it is human beings who are the high point of God's creation, uniquely created in his image as they are, and that animals come, very much, in second place. If animals can serve human beings, this view holds, then they are at least useful for that.

However, many Christians would be surprised to learn this. Their natural instincts and their Christian compassion tell them differently. Any interaction they have, or have had, with animals will urge them to question this received teaching. They might even be quite shocked to discover such a thing. Whilst they do not need to move away from the of-course-humans-have-dominion view, they would mostly want to understand this God-given authority in terms of a caring and compassionate oversight of the planet and of every existing being. The idea that animals are not deserving of love or care, or that they are only to be seen as valuable in terms of their usefulness to humans, could seem cold and offensive. It's simply not where most people are. Even those who don't claim to have much emotional investment in animals may find this view unreflective of a generally received natural human instinct: to care for and to protect the vulnerable and the needy.

It is not necessary to like animals in order to argue that they have value and worth over and above their usefulness to humans. Indeed, a responsible Christian view would surely say that animals are deserving of respect and care, and a sense of being treated well, in and of their own right; that care and consideration for animals is derived from natural law (a God-given and innate sense in human beings about what is right and wrong), and so part of the moral order of the universe. Those Christians who struggle with the view that animals deserve kindness in their own right, must at least see that God has the right to have them treated appropriately? If humans deliberately treat animals with harshness or cruelty, it is logically acceptable to argue that it's not the rights of animals which are violated, but that the action of cruelty itself is in direct conflict with the order and design of God the creator.

Without departing from the teaching of the church, even in the smallest way, we understand that Christians naturally acknowledge animals as having been created by God and will need to render to God an account for their treatment of them. After all, being made in the image of God, perhaps humans are challenged also to behave more like God, not least to each other and to animals. To care for animals, indeed, and to promote their welfare is a godly act, surely, since it is to contribute to the restoration of a fallen creation, longing for the reestablishing of the peaceable kingdom as first created by God in the garden of Eden.

We can also say that, because in Jesus we see one who became a servant (evidenced by his setting aside the glory of heaven to become flesh in the womb of the Virgin, his birth in a cave, his humble entrance into Jerusalem on a donkey, his death on the cross, among other examples), and in whom St. Paul tells us is the freely chosen form of servanthood (Phil 2:7), and whom Isaiah prophecies is the righteous servant (Isa 11:5; 53:11), we worship a Servant-God; that Jesus, who is our way to heaven, in whom we find everything we need (and so much more), and who divests himself of heavenly glory and shows us how to be servants to one another, is also the Jesus in whose image and likeness we are made. We are a race called to serve and to minister to those around us (including animals) with compassion and gentleness, modelling the life of Jesus himself.

To put it even more directly and succinctly, we worship a Servant God and so, being made in his image, we are, specifically and uniquely, the servant species. To serve is to model (and to become) Jesus himself. It is in pouring ourselves out for others that we discover who we truly are. Because animals are so dependent upon humans for kindness and compassion, there is, perhaps, a kind of priority in serving them and, in doing so, to be reminded that all life, created and inspired by God himself, is worthy of honour and respect. I can't help believing, as a Christian, that because it is so easy to control, abuse, and dishonour animals, the call to *avoid* that possibility is even greater. After all, Christians believe in the Shepherd who gives his own life for the sheep—not the other way around (John 10:11)!

Cardinal Arthur Hinsley (1865–1943), one-time Archbishop of Westminster, famously said that "cruelty to animals is the degrading attitude of paganism,"[1] heavily suggesting that, for Christians, there is another way: a way of benevolence and mercy which is expressed to all living beings. One of his predecessors at Westminster, Cardinal Edward Manning (1808–1892), an implacable opposer of vivisection at a time when such a custom was normalised and taken for granted, was more specific: "We owe a sevenfold obligation to the Creator of those animals. Our obligation and moral duty is to him who made them and, if we wish to know the limit and broad outline of our obligation, I say at once it is his nature, his perfections—and, among those perfections, is most profoundly that of eternal mercy. Although a poor mule, or poor horse is not, indeed, a moral person, yet the Lord and maker of the mule is the highest lawgiver, and his nature is a law unto himself. In giving a dominion over his creatures to man, he gave it subject to the condition that it should be used in conformity to his perfections which is his own law, and therefore our law."[2]

Cardinal John Heenan (1905–1975), too, says that "it was once pointed out that the Catechism had no question about cruelty to animals or, indeed, to children. The difficulty is that many people do not realise the extent to which cruelty to animals is practised as a matter of business.... The rights of God can be transgressed through ignorance as well as malice.... Christians have a duty not only to refrain from doing harm but also to do positive good."[3] Addressing all Christians, the cardinal calls for an understanding of animals within the context of charity and mercy, and of truly noticing the ways in which they are treated by society. He is quite clear

---

1. Hinsley, sermon, 1889, Wynne-Tyson, *Extended Circle*, 387, cited in Linzey and Regan, *Compassion*, 47.
2. *Zoophilist*, cited in Linzey and Regan, *Compassion*, 47.
3. Agius, *God's Animals*, 3.

What about the Popes?

that a lack of awareness concerning current practices (or refusing to see, we might say), is no excuse!

Pope Benedict XVI was well-known as an animal lover (he also famously loved Fanta and Mozart). There are many photographs around with him smiling happily, whilst nursing a cat on his lap. He, most likely, will have enjoyed the popular and amusing view expressing the vast difference between dogs and cats: Rex the dog believes that, because all his needs are met by humans, humans must be gods; Jenny the cat, on the other hand, believes that because all her needs are met by humans, *she* must be God!

What of the popes and animals? Have they held particular views though the ages? As Clair Linzey points out in her *Developing Animal Theology*, there is a not a single mention of animals in all the documents of Vatican II.[4] That seems extraordinary and surprising, when the church was, at that time, seeking to embrace the world in a new way and to share the treasures of the faith by engaging with people in their ordinary, everyday situations. What of all those out there who believe that animals matter? Or those who want to see the place of animals in God's creation addressed?

Some outstanding theologians, Catholic and otherwise, have been contributing to, and developing, the arguments concerning an appropriate Christian understanding of animals in recent years, and have challenged us to think again. The church is, I'm sure, willing to hear these carefully considered views. A look at the popes may help us get a context for some official teachings of the church concerning animals.

Popes have been keen, through the ages, to bless the work of animal welfare projects and events. These include Pius II (1458–1464), who wrote stories about his dog Musetta; Paul II (1464–1471), who loved to bless animals and award golden coins to his favourites; Pius V (1566–1572), who emphatically declared that bullfighting was an unworthy pursuit for Catholics; Pius IX (1846–1878), who was well-known for his huge papal menagerie; Leo XIII (1878–1903), who is remembered for the exotic creatures he brought to live at the Vatican; Benedict XV (1914–1922), who included animals in his pleas for peace and well-being during his diplomatic attempts in World War I; Pius XI (1922–1939), who, in his famous encyclical *Casti Connubi* of 1939, mentions the moral duty to treat animals humanely; Pius XII (1939–1958), a huge fan of companion animals who enjoyed having birds and dogs to share the Vatican with him; John XXIII (1958–1963), who declared that for every creature there must be respect

---

4. Linzey, *Developing Animal Theology*, 119.

and care because God has created them; Paul VI (1963–1978) who touches on the ethical treatment of animals in his 1968 encyclical *Humane Vitae*; John Paul II (1978–2005), who is well documented in calling for kindness and respect towards animals; Benedict XVI (2005–2013), who advocates for the compassionate treatment of animals within the context of environmental stewardship, and, of course, the current Holy Father. That is a significant list and says something about the importance that the popes historically have placed on animals in the life of the church and the world. Naturally, no pope has ever endorsed cruelty to animals or stated that such cruelty is without moral concern. Many popes throughout history have clearly viewed animals as deserving of protection and care.

To cite a specific example of the influence of Rome, Pope Benedict XV, as mentioned above, confirmed (in 1920) the church's opposition to bull fighting. Revisiting a former proclamation by one of his predecessors,[5] he roundly declared the mind of the church as being "altogether in the spirit of our Holy Books, which call even on wild animals to bless the good God, and wholly accords with the gentle law of Him Who has deigned to call Himself the Lamb of God. . . . If, in spite of the spirit of humanity which the New Law encourages, human savagery falls away again in the promotion of bullfights, there is no doubt that the church continues, as she has done in the past, loudly to condemn these shameful and bloody spectacles."[6]

To take the first of just a few more modern examples; in 1950, Pope Pius XII said that "the animal world, as with all of creation, is a manifestation of God's power, his wisdom, his goodness—and, as such, deserves human respect and consideration. Any reckless desire to kill off animals, and all unnecessary harshness and callous cruelty towards them is to be condemned."[7]

Much later, in 1990, at a general audience, as we have previously noted, but in a comment worthy of repetition, Pope John Paul II said, "[Biblical] texts admit that even animals have a breath of life, received from God. Under this aspect, man, having come forth from the hands of God, appears in solidarity with all living beings."[8] In saying this, Pope St. John Paul II underlines the reality that animals share, with humans, the "breath of life"

---

5. Pius V, *De Salute Gregis Dominici*.

6. Letter of Cardinal Gasparri, in the name of the pope, to the Toulon Branch of the Society for the Protection of Animals (see Gasparri, "Creation Is Disposed").

7. Pius XII, "Structure of the Matter," §2.

8. John Paul II, "Udienza Generale," §5.

received from the creator, and that God sustains all life in existence. This is, indeed, the work of the Spirit, the Lord of Life.

During a pilgrimage to Assisi in 1982, Pope John Paul II had stated that "St. Francis is before us as an example of unalterable meekness and sincere love with regard to the irrational beings who make up part of creation."[9] Whilst asserting the traditional Catholic view of the irrationality of animals, his thrust is such that these animals (perhaps even more *as a result* of their irrationality) deserve sincere kindness and charity—not least because they are part of God's creation. In the same address, he went on to say, "Created in the image of God, we [human beings] must make him [God] present among creatures [animals] 'as intelligent and noble masters and guardians of nature, and not as heedless exploiters and destroyers.'"

Later, in his *Sollicitudo Rei Socialis* of 1988, Pope John Paul II would make the startling and exciting claim that there is a need among Catholics and all Christians to honour and respect "the nature of each being," going further and saying categorically that the God-given "dominion granted to man ... is not an absolute power, nor can one speak of freedom to 'use and misuse', or to dispose of things as one pleases."[10] This supports the view previously cited, that dominion is often considered a kind of stewardship—a shared obligation for the maintaining of the harmony originally inherent in God's creation. Those who have that dominion have a particular responsibility to uphold, in God's name (because made in his image), that harmony. The Holy Father further confirms this view in 1995 with *Evangelium Vitae*: "As one called to till and look after the garden of the world (*Genesis 2:15*), man has a specific responsibility towards the environment in which he lives, towards the creation which God has put at the service of his personal dignity, of his life, not only for the present but also for future generations."[11]

The animal-loving Pope Benedict XVI has also had interesting things to say about animals and their relationship both with the world and with humans. In a 2002 interview about the rights and wrongs of eating animals, he made this now well-quoted assertion: "We can see that they [the animals] are given into our care, and that we cannot just do whatever we want with them. Animals, too, are God's creatures. . . . Certainly, a sort of industrial use of creatures, so that geese are fed in such a way as to produce as large a liver as possible, hens live so packed together that they become

---

9. John Paul II, "To the People of Assisi," §5.
10. John Paul II, *Sollicitudo Rei Socialis*, §34.
11. John Paul II, *Evangelium Vitae*, §42.

just caricatures of birds; this degrading of living creatures to a commodity seems to me in fact to contradict the relationship of mutuality that comes across in the Bible."[12]

While this remains a personal view of Cardinal Ratzinger, who, at that time, was head of the Congregation for the Doctrine of the Faith (perhaps the most senior Vatican appointment after the Holy Father), later, as Pope Benedict XVI, he was to say more, including indirect references to animals: "The Church has a responsibility towards creation . . . as [a] gift [that] God the Creator meant for everyone."[13]

Talking about St. Francis of Assisi, Benedict XVI said:

> From love for Christ stems love for others and also for all of God's creatures. This is yet another characteristic trait of Francis' spirituality: the sense of universal brotherhood and love for creation, which inspired the famous *Canticle of Creatures*. This too is an extremely timely message. As I recalled in my recent Encyclical *Caritas in Veritate*, development is sustainable only when it respects creation and does not damage the environment, and in the *Message for the World Day of Peace* this year (2010), I also underscored that even building stable peace is linked to respect for creation. St. Francis reminds us that the wisdom and benevolence of the Creator is expressed through creation. He understood nature as a language in which God speaks to us, in which reality becomes clear, and we can speak *of* God and *with* God.[14]

Animals are a part of God's creation and, as such, are a gift from God for whom we humans have a direct responsibility.

Then there's Pope Francis. In *Lumen Fidei* (2013), an encyclical which the two popes (Benedict XVI and Francis) wrote together, it is stated that "at the heart of Biblical faith is God's love, his concrete concern for every person, and his plan of salvation which embraces all of humanity and *all creation*, culminating in the incarnation, death and resurrection of Jesus Christ."[15] Here the text appears to suggest that the birth, death, and resurrection of Jesus somehow has a transformative effect not just for humans but for all of creation. It is a fundamental option to believe that the Christ-event is not confined just to human beings, but has an eternal significance

---

12. Ratzinger, *God and the World*, 78–79.
13. Benedict XVI, "World Day of Peace" (2010), §12.
14. Benedict XVI, "General Audience," §14.
15. Francis, *Lumen Fidei*, §54; my emphasis.

for animals, and for all other aspects of creation too, as suggested in previous chapters. The life, death, and resurrection of Jesus makes a difference for all life.

I have quoted extensively from *Laudato Si'*, the 2015 encyclical of Pope Francis, throughout this book. Revisiting those quotations and the whole document reminds us of the shift which is gradually taking place in the church, from a human-centred understanding of creation towards a more human-and-creaturely-together-centred view. In this wider view, humans have a role, of course, and remain those endowed with unique gifts from God, but animals (and the whole of the rest of the created order) have a role too. When the various elements live together in a divinely designed harmony, humans, animals, and plants will flourish again as God intended.

On October 4, 2023, Pope Francis published a companion document to *Laudato Si'*. *Laudate Deum* is a cry from the heart of the pope for the world to stop destroying itself and for the human race to finally take responsibility for the destruction which has been caused. Pope Francis includes the animal world to some extent in this very contemporary exposition. The first words of the apostolic exhortation are "praise God for all his creatures," and is an obvious reference to Francis of Assisi's "Canticle." An encouraging start. The pope then mentions how the world is becoming damaged and warns of the terrifying reality that "other creatures of this world have stopped becoming our companions along the way and have instead become our victims."[16]

Warning about human beings narrow-mindedly assuming absolute control over the planet, in section 21, Pope Francis says that humans have been obsessed: "To increase human power beyond anything imaginable, before which nonhuman reality is a mere resource at its disposal. Everything that exists ceases to be a gift for which we should be thankful, esteem and cherish, and instead becomes a slave, prey to any whim of the human mind and its capacities." The "nonhuman reality" to which the pope refers here must surely mean animals and all other forms of life on earth.[17] Many of those with concerns for animal welfare would certainly suggest that, to please ourselves, humans have indeed caused God's creatures to "become a slave" which is prey to the whims and shortcomings of human control.

---

16. Francis, *LD*, §16.
17. Francis, *LD*, §21.

In a section entitled *Spiritual Motivations*, Pope Francis reminds us that "God has united us to all his creatures,"[18] and that "responsibility for God's earth means that human beings, endowed with intelligence, must respect the laws of nature and the delicate equilibria existing between the creatures of this world."[19] He also reminds us that "human life is incomprehensible and unsustainable without other creatures." For "as part of the universe . . . all of us are linked by unseen bonds and together form a kind of universal family, a sublime communion which fills us with a sacred, affectionate and humble respect.""[20] The Holy Father concludes this short document with the bold statement: "'Praise God' is the title of this letter for, when human beings claim to take God's place, they become their own worst enemies."[21] Indeed.

It is perhaps time for us to take on board, more consciously, the importance of treating animals well. Maybe it is even our Christian duty. Is it possible that God deserves and requires it of us? As we have seen, many of the popes appear to think so.

Laudato Si, Pope Francis

> The created things of this world are not free of ownership: "For they are yours, O Lord, who love the living" (*Wis 11:26*). This is the basis of our conviction that, as part of the universe, called into being by one Father, all of us are linked by unseen bonds and together form a kind of universal family, a sublime communion which fills us with a sacred, affectionate and humble respect. Here I would reiterate that "God has joined us so closely to the world around us that we can feel the desertification of the soil almost as a physical ailment, and the extinction of a species as a painful disfigurement."[22]

---

18. Francis, *LD*, §66.
19. Francis, *LD*, §62, quoting the Special Assembly for the Pan-Amazonian region, 2019.
20. Francis, *LD*, §67, quoting *LS*.
21. Francis, *LD*, §73.
22. Francis, *LS*, §89.

Prayer

We praise you, O God, for your glory displayed in all the creatures of the earth . . .
for all things exist only as seen by you, only as known by you . . .
They affirm you in living: all things affirm you in living;
the bird in the air, both the hawk and the finch;
the beast on the earth, both the wolf and the lamb;
Through Jesus Christ our Lord. Amen.

(T. S. Eliot)[23]

---

23. Eliot, *Murder in the Cathedral*, cited in Linzey and Regan, *Compassion*, 13.

14

Why Are There So Many Stories and Legends Associated with Saints?

Noah opened the window of the ark that he had made and sent forth a raven. It went to and fro until the waters were dried up from the earth. Then he sent forth a dove from him, to see if the waters had subsided from the face of the ground. But the dove found no place to set her foot, and she returned to him to the ark, for the waters were still on the face of the whole earth. So he put out his hand and took her and brought her into the ark with him. He waited another seven days, and again he sent forth the dove out of the ark. And the dove came back to him in the evening, and behold, in her mouth was a freshly plucked olive leaf! So Noah knew that the waters had subsided from the earth.

(Genesis 8:6–11)

A SAINT, OF COURSE, is a holy person—someone who, by their life and bearing, points beyond themself and, instead, to God. To meet a saint is to come away feeling that we have truly encountered the divine. God obviously works with the reality of whom he has created: each human being, unique and individual, filled with the potential for holiness. In fact, to become holy is to become more Christlike, and to become more Christlike is to become everything that we have been created to be.

Why Are There So Many Stories and Legends Associated with Saints?

I know a saint. I don't mean a saint who has been recognised as such by the church, or who has been proclaimed officially holy by the pope. This person is still living and still concerned with the teaching and preaching of the gospel. Whenever I meet him, I am impressed by his humility and selflessness but, more than that, I kind of want to be like him. I don't mean like him in terms of his personality, but I feel a deep invitation from the Lord, when I have spent time with this person, to imitate his holiness. He would be horrified to know that I felt this way and would be the first to denounce me for promoting such fantasy and craziness. But that's part of his holiness. God has been good to the saints in that he doesn't reveal to them the remarkable holiness and faithfulness of their lives, lest the sins of pride and conceit take away the very graces of which they are unaware.

If each of us is called to be a saint, each of us, in aspiring to be holy, has that God-given potential within us. God would not ask of us something which he cannot, with our cooperation, make a reality. We are created by a God of complete holiness, and we bear within us his own image, so it must be possible. You are called to holiness: the holiness of a Francis of Assisi or a Benedict of Nursia or a Teresa of Calcutta. Indeed, by God's grace, you have within you the potential to outdo these and other saints by the power of the Holy Spirit at work in you. St. John of the Cross (1542–1591) famously declared, "Remember always that you came here for no other reason than to be a saint; thus let nothing reign in your soul which does not lead you to sanctity."[1] In the context of the vocation to be authentically holy, we have seen that many of the saints intuitively understood that associating with animals was a positive and practical way to grow in holiness.

Animals, too, could be thought to have some kind of divine potential within them, since they, like us, find their origin and their destiny in the God who created them. The church does not, of course, officially say that animals can be holy, but if we look at the lives of the saints through history, and at the relationships that many of the saints have had with animals, we can see that there is a certain similarity: the pursuit of holiness for humans and the example and companionship of animals has always been there. God is presumably saying something to us, through these stories and legends about how much animals, within the context of creation, are not only valued, but that they can teach us humans a thing or two—even, perhaps, how to live gospel values in a real way and to perceive, in the whole of creation, something of the goodness, the grandeur, and the generosity of God.

---

1. John of the Cross, *Collected Works*, 16.

I would go so far as to say that there is a deep and sacred bond between saints (and all holy people) and animals. David Clough suggests that when we look at the connection between human sanctity and animals, we see that the two go together to reveal a "recognition that it belongs to Christian holiness to be friendly towards animals, [to have] a high view of the capacities of animals to be responsive subjects, and an appreciation that God's will is for peace between all creatures. Together with many other examples . . . such as St. Jerome's hospitality to the lion, or St. Godric's protection of a stag from the Durham Prince Bishop's hunt, it shows that Christians have long recognised that Christian holiness has implications well beyond the human realm."[2]

St. Antony of Padua, he of the "jewelled" preaching at the Papal Court and a renowned follower of St. Francis of Assisi, is usually considered to be the saint on whom we call when we lose or misplace important items and objects. I have invoked him in this way on many occasions. His connection with animals, however, while less well known, is equally intriguing. Legend has it that when those professing untruths about the Catholic faith crudely questioned the wisdom of the church's teaching and refused to listen to St. Antony's orthodox preaching, he turned away from them and instead towards the sea. It is recorded that miraculously, when he did, a multitude of fish gathered near the shore, their heads lifted up, as if in attentive and thoughtful prayer and praise. Authentic, honest preaching turns the heads of even the fishes.

Legends exist for a reason, whether they testify to historical truth or not. The reason here could be that St. Antony was well respected for his innate ability to relate to these God-created animals, and that this story demonstrates the much-received truth that he perceived in a profound way the interconnectedness of the whole of God's creation. We might say that this is not unlike Pope Francis today, especially in his teaching from *Laudato Si'* and *Laudate Deum*. It is notable that it was sea creatures and fishes that listened to St. Antony—a species which is so often considered less valuable and less important than other animals because of apparent (probably incorrect) beliefs about their lack of sentience and, therefore, their lack of ability to feel pain. Modern science questions these assumptions and, for believers so, it appears, does St. Antony.

Another popular saint is the Peruvian St. Martin de Porres. He is revered for his humility and for living well the virtue of compassion,

---

2. Clough, "Animals: Who Cares?," §13.

expressed not just towards humans, but to all living beings. Famously, St. Martin could not walk past injured and suffering animals and went out of his way to care for them and, wherever possible, to nurture them back to full health. As well as being one of the official patron saints of animals, he is said to have been gifted by God with the ability to heal, and to perform miraculous cures. Perhaps some of the animals across which he came benefited from these extraordinary graces. He is particularly well remembered for the legend of the rats. "It is told that the prior, who objected to rats, ordered Martin to set out poison for them. Martin did as he was asked but was very sorry for the rats. He went out into the garden, called softly, and out came the rats. He reprimanded them for their bad habits, telling them about the poison. He further assured them that he would feed them every day in the garden, if they would refrain from annoying the prior. This agreed upon, he dismissed the rats and forever after, so the stories go, there was no more trouble with rats at Holy Rosary Convent."[3]

St. Martin exemplifies for us the now very familiar and valuable Catholic/biblical notion of dominion, emphasising the importance of a responsible and compassionate care for all of God's creation, the large and the small. Surely the God who does not overlook the needs of the sparrow (Matt 10:31) will not fail to see the needs of each of his creatures.

Moving beyond the scope of the Catholic tradition, it may be helpful to explore another wise and profound part of Christianity, the eastern orthodox churches. St. Seraphim of Sarov is usually remembered for his spiritual wisdom and teaching, as well as his asceticism (what we can understand as a healthy form of self-discipline, practised out of love for Jesus). His life and teachings, as we might expect, extend beyond the eastern orthodox world to Christians of all traditions. It is reported that St. Seraphim had a special bond with animals, and according to local accounts of his life, would seek out and feed wild bears and wolves when they came to him, in the midst of the cold Russian wilderness. His kindness and care for these large, frightening animals reminds us of the important harmony which God desires for his world between all of humanity and all of his natural order. Seraphim "preached to the animals, shared his food with them, and is especially known for taming the bear and wolves in his area. His friendship with the animals of the forest was a source of wonder to visitors and even to his

---

3. Dorcy, *St. Dominic's Family*, 483.

fellow monks and, according to eyewitnesses, rabbits, foxes, lynx, lizards and even the bears and wolves gathered peacefully around his simple hut."[4]

In a theological document entitled *Communion and Stewardship: Human Persons Created in the Image of God* of 2004, the church unsurprisingly asserts the ontological difference between animals and humans but, at the same time, says that "animals are the creatures of God, and, according to the Scriptures, he surrounds them with his providential care (*Matthew 6:26*). Human beings should accept them with gratitude and, even adopting a eucharistic attitude with regard to every element of creation, to give thanks to God for them," and then goes on to make the beautiful and challenging statement that "the harmony which man must establish, or restore, in the whole of creation includes his relationship to the animals. When Christ comes in his glory, he will 'recapitulate' the whole of creation in an eschatological and definitive moment of harmony."[5] The saints intuitively understand the call to adopt a "eucharistic attitude" to animals and they show us that authentic holiness celebrates the essential role and place of animals in God's good creation.

I have long had a devotion to St. Richard of Chichester (1197–1253). He is, after all, a former bishop of the diocese in which I live. He was known for his assiduous care of the clergy and for his cheerful countenance. He was also outspoken on behalf of animals: "Poor innocent little creatures [to animals bound for slaughter]: if you were reasoning beings and could speak you would curse us. For we are the cause of your death, and what have you done to deserve it?"[6] It is a sobering thought, even today, so many years after the saint first said it.

The deep and moving connection between saints and animals is a thought-provoking and captivating part of our Christian spirituality underscoring, as it does, the treasured belief that all of creation, because it comes from God himself, is both interconnected and worthy of reverence. Examples from saints like Francis of Assisi, Antony of Padua, Martin de Porres, Seraphim of Sarov, and so many others draw us to recall, again and again, the importance of humility, compassion and stewardship in our relationship with the animal kingdom. These saints are not just wonderful spiritual guides (for whom we thank God), but also champions and promoters

---

4. Orthodox Fellowship of the Transfiguration, "St. Seraphim," §1.
5. International Theological Commission, *Communion and Stewardship*, §79.
6. Butler, *Butler's Lives*, 2:24.

of the need for a harmonious coexistence between human beings and the many and diverse creatures with which we share our beautiful world.

Laudato Si', Pope Francis

> By learning to see and appreciate beauty, we learn to reject self-interested pragmatism. If someone has not learned to stop and admire something beautiful, we should not be surprised if he or she treats everything as an object to be used and abused without scruple.[7]

Prayer

O merciful Father, who has given life to all things,
and who love all that you have made,
pour into our hearts the spirit of your own loving kindness,
that we may show mercy to helpless creatures
and glorify you by that gentleness which is in accordance with your holy will.
Through Jesus Christ our Lord. Amen.

(William Carter)[8]

---

7. Francis, *LS*, §215.
8. Cited in Linzey and Regan, *Compassion*, 71.

15

Is an Authentic View of Animals Continuing to Develop and Grow within the Church?

Let the heavens be glad, and let the earth rejoice;
let the sea roar, and all that fills it;
let the field exult, and everything in it!

(PSALM 96:11–12)

AT A RECENT GATHERING of priests, it was interesting to note just how many of the brethren mentioned their companion animals, often remarking that the friendship, affection and humour that these animals bring make a significant contribution to maintaining good mental health and well-being for the priest concerned. This is certainly true for me. My bishop sometimes jokingly refers to me as "Master of Hounds" (however uncomfortable the allusion to fox hunting makes me). As he knows, I make no apology for talking about my dogs ad infinitum, and for taking out my mobile phone at every opportunity to share photos of them. Many of the priests present at the meeting live and work in challenging circumstances, often having to manage big, busy parishes on their own and without much domestic or emotional support. We all do our best and, it must be said, are constantly appreciative of our amazing parishioners who (for the most part) give us unending support and encouragement. But our beloved companion animals really make a difference too. I know from my pastoral encounters over many years that for our parishioners, the animals with whom they share their homes and lives mean so much; more, probably, than we can realistically quantify. Our companion animals are part of the family and are worthy of important consideration when we make decisions about how we live our busy lives. I could not, for example, imagine going on holiday to a place where I couldn't have my dogs accompany me. It would be unthinkable to leave them behind while I went off for a jolly. Those who, for whatever reason, are not able to offer homes to domestic animals still find, in the beauty of the natural world around them, real delight and pleasure in free-living birds and insects and a multitude of other creatures.

Humphrey Primatt (1734–1776) was an Anglican clergyman who concerned himself with issues like animal rights and the particular responsibilities of Christians to treat animals well. In his *Dissertation on the Duty of Mercy and Sin of Cruelty to Brute Animals*,[1] he set a new standard for understanding a human-animal relationship under God. In this work, he argues forcefully that all animals have been created by God and, therefore, any form of cruelty to animals is a kind of atheism. He went further when he stated that "pain is pain, whether it be inflicted on man or on beast."[2] Primatt was one of several influential commentators and patrons of a social movement concerned with animal welfare. In fact, the RSPCA would later declare that his writing was a foundation stone of their entire purpose and mission. A champion of evangelicals, Primatt's influence has contributed to a sea-change in society's perception on animals and who they are. "We may pretend to what religion we please; but cruelty is atheism," he said. "We may make our boast of Christianity; but cruelty is infidelity. We may trust to our orthodoxy; but cruelty is the worst of heresies."[3]

As previously noted, we live today in what many would consider are enlightened times. The buzzwords in contemporary employment and in wider society are terms like inclusion, respect, diversity, and equality. There is a desire to afford people the respect which is rightly their due. No one, least of all a Christian, would suggest that, for example, slavery has a place in modern society, or that women should be treated as inferior to men. These developments (which, obviously still have some way to go) have, as we know, swept through society and there is much media heat around how we live these concepts appropriately and fairly. But it all sounds and feels

---

1. Primatt, *Dissertation*.
2. Primatt, *Dissertation*, 269.
3. Primatt, *Dissertation*, 321.

rather anthropocentric; it's all about men and women; it only concerns itself with human beings. Very little thought is generally given to animals, and they are still usually (and legally, very often) seen just as property and utilities, judged only by their usefulness to humans.

Last summer, my dog Georgie, who's a keen hunter, was preoccupied with a wasp as I sat, with a visiting friend, in the garden. Georgie was chasing and bothering the wasp endlessly. This seemed to irritate the person who was with me, who thought nothing of promptly going over and stamping on the wasp as a way of bringing Georgie's behaviour to an end. After all, it's only an insect, and an irritating one at that, she probably thought. This is a good and kind person but someone who has, like you and me, been shaped by the attitudes and mores of society, especially around animals. Another, much more recent, example occurred in a conversation with a friend who was describing an event with his sister's dog. "It jumped up onto her lap and instantly died," he said incredulously. Every time an animal is described as an "it," a particular attitude is revealed. The animal about whom he was speaking was a much loved "he" or "she," not an "it." She was no mere property or fashion accessory; she was a treasured member of the family who, in her own lived experience, understood happiness and sadness, felt the cold in winter and the warmth in summer, and so on.

The church is somewhat on the move in these matters, but we Catholics are, of course, as shaped and formed by the prevailing attitudes of society as everyone else.

I have already reflected on the evidence that many of the popes, through the history of the church, have had an awareness of the role of animals in God's plan for the world. Some of the popes have called for animals to be treated with kindness and compassion. The animals are, after all, part of God's creation too. Before that we saw that St. Thomas Aquinas, heavily influenced by Aristotle, had an instrumental view of animals, suggesting that they are not deserving of moral worth because they are, in his philosophical terms, irrational. René Descartes went further in suggesting that any screaming that animals might make when subjected to violence, were merely the noises of machinery breaking down. Some modern theologians have upheld and supported these views (often by implication), and this has led to a sense that only human beings matter; indeed, that humans beings alone can have a relationship with God, because they alone are like God. Perhaps to say that only human beings matter is to say, equally, that animals *do not* matter; that, because animals are deemed (in this context) not worthy of theological distinction, ergo they are not worthy of human interest. Throughout this book, I have been trying to say that it is time for a more developed view and that Scripture, and the slowly emerging tradition of the church, can provide a different, renewed perspective for us.

In his beautiful encyclical *Sollicitudo Rei Socialis* of 1988, as we have seen, Pope John Paul II hints at the beginnings of a departure from the old instrumentalist view of animals, suggesting that, within creation, it is important to respect "the nature of each being" and that "the dominion granted to man . . . is not an absolute power, nor can one speak of freedom to 'use and misuse,' or to dispose of things as one pleases."[4] To today's Catholic, that doesn't sound like a particularly extraordinary thing to say, and many would happily agree with the sentiments expressed, yet there continues to be a sense, in lived fact, that animals are perceived as objects and are instrumentalised by the church and by many Catholics and other Christians. I hesitate to mention, for example, bullfighting in Spain, France, and Asia, or even fox or stag hunting in the UK, which still continues, even though it is illegal, where animals are obviously seen as mere objects used entirely and cruelly for the entertainment of humans, and at great cost to the safety and well-being of the animals themselves. Pope St. John Paul's II's words invite us to reconsider, from an ethical perspective, such a view of animals.

Anticipating much of what Pope Francis will say even more clearly in *Laudato Si'*, the catechism says, "The seventh commandment ('You shall not steal,' *Exodus 20:15*) enjoins respect for the integrity of creation. Animals, like plants and inanimate beings, are by nature destined for the common good of past, present and future humanity. . . . Man's dominion over inanimate and other living beings granted by the Creator is not absolute; it is limited by concern for the quality of life of his neighbour, including generations to come; it requires a religious aspect for the integrity of creation."[5] Human beings have a responsibility to care for all the different elements of creation, including animals, as a responsible steward and as a gift to future generations.

Pope St. John Paul II presented the church with an exciting encyclical (thus forming part of the official teaching of the church) in 1995. *Evangelium Vitae* is the pope's call for a recognition of the sanctity of human life, specifically, but does not exclude the reverence due to other forms of life.

---

4. John Paul II, *Sollicitudo Rei Socialis*, §34.
5. *CCC*, §2415.

"It is the ecological question—ranging from the preservation of the natural habitats of different species of animals and of other forms of life ... which finds in the Bible clear and strong ethical direction, leading to a solution which respects the great good of life, of every life."[6]

I have already mentioned Pope Benedict XVI's call (when he was still Cardinal Ratzinger) for a reconsideration of the animals who suffer so terribly in factory farming. As Pope, however, he was also clear: "The Church has a responsibility towards creation, and she considers it her duty to exercise that responsibility in public life, in order to protect the earth, water and air, as gifts of God the Creator meant for everyone, and above all to save mankind from the danger of self-destruction."[7] Animals are clearly the gifts of God and, as such, need to be considered as part of the responsibility which humankind has towards the whole of creation.

At his inaugural address, following his election, Pope Francis said, in 2013, "[The vocation of being a protector] means protecting all of creation, the beauty of the created world, as the Book of Genesis and as St. Francis of Assisi showed us. It means respecting each of God's creatures and respecting the environment in which we live."[8] This statement, groundbreaking and refreshing in its clarity and novelty, shows a gradual but welcome shift in the thinking and the theology of the church's view of animals and of creation in general. No pope, or Vatican document, or official teaching of the church, has so specifically and clearly called on humans to "protect" other creatures and the planet in such a way. Pope Francis, as shown in the many references to the document in this book, crystallises and develops much of that thinking in *Laudato Si'*.

Francis goes further and, in the early days of his pontificate says, when speaking again of creation, "[Subjugation] does not mean to exploit [creation], but to cultivate and guard it, to care for it with [human] labour. Work is part of the plan of God's love; we are called to cultivate and safeguard all the goods of creation and in this way we participate in the work of creation."[9]

We can see that there's an emerging picture, a gradual change in the awareness and sensitivity of the church, through her official pronouncements, to creation, and to animals.

6. John Paul II, *Evangelium Vitae*, §42.
7. Benedict XVI, "World Day of Peace" (2010), §12.
8. Francis, "Mass," §6.
9. Francis, "General Audience," §3.

Is an Authentic View of Animals Continuing to Develop and Grow within the Church?

More recently, in response to *Laudato Si'*, the Catholic Bishops' Conference of England and Wales produced *The Call of Creation*.[10] Originally produced in 2002, and then updated and reissued, it is a document that invites Catholics, other Christians, indeed all people, to respond with urgency to the current environmental crisis. In setting the context, the document immediately recalls Pope Francis: "The world, created according to the divine model, is a web of relationships. Creatures tend towards God, and in turn it is proper to every living being to tend towards other things. . . . This leads us not only to marvel at the manifold connections existing among creatures, but also to discover a key to our own fulfilment. The human person grows more, matures more, and is sanctified more, to the extent that he or she enters into relationships, going out from themselves to live in communion with God, with others and with all creatures."[11]

In the foreword to *The Call of Creation*, Bishop John Arnold and Bishop Richard Moth remind readers that there is no such thing as small, insignificant actions when looking to resolve the climate emergency through which we are currently living. Each of us can make a difference: "Individual choices can seem insignificant when faced with major global challenges. But Pope Francis has rightly stated that multiplied individual actions can indeed make a real difference. As individual children of God, it is important that we think carefully about how we use consumer goods and value simplicity in our lives. We should also care for, and nurture, that part of God's creation for which we are particularly responsible. By doing this, collectively, as brothers and sisters in Christ, we can also help to change our culture."[12] Choosing not to commodify or instrumentalise animals; thinking carefully about how we, as human beings, use (or don't use) animals for food, clothing, sport, entertainment and so on, can contribute significantly to the change in the world that we all want to see.

The Call of Creation also reminds us of what the great St. Ambrose of Milan (374–397), drawing on the Gospel of St. Luke, said in the fourth century: "If God's providence bestows an unfailing supply of food on the birds of the air who neither sow nor reap, we ought to realise that the reason for people's supply running short is human greed. The fruits of the earth were given to feed all without distinction and nobody can claim any particular rights. Instead, we have lost the sense of the communion of goods, rushing

---

10. CBCEW, *Call of Creation*.
11. Francis, *LS*, §240.
12. CBCEW, *Call of Creation*, 2–3.

to turn these goods into private property."[13] When we perceive animals only as objects for our own use, rather than as creatures of the living God, we turn them into private property and end up feeding our own greed even more.

The bishops cannot avoid reflecting on the need for a return to the vision of the peaceable kingdom and a sense that, if the planet is to be saved from catastrophe, animals must be given the proper respect and care that they deserve: "The loss of species is undeniable and, with this loss of species, our need for beauty and our communion with the other creatures of the earth are denied."[14] Unless we live in harmony and unity with the other species of the earth, not dominating them but reverencing and protecting them, we will undo our own call to live authentically and honestly.

Chapter 3 sees the Bishops' Conference referencing Pope St. John Paul II. The great pope says, in *Redemptor Hominis*, "Man often seems to see no other meaning in his natural environment than what serves for immediate use and consumption. Yet it was the Creator's will that man should communicate with nature as an intelligent and noble 'master' and 'guardian', and not as a heedless 'exploiter' and 'destroyer.'"[15] When we see animals as objects for our own use, and fail to recognise within them the divine, we exploit and destroy them and, in so doing, end up exploiting and destroying ourselves.

The bishops go on to remind us again of the importance given by the catechism to all created things: "We believe that God is the Creator of everything there is, and that this creation is good, reflecting God's own goodness (*Genesis 1-2*). Each creature possesses its own particular goodness and perfection. For each one of the works of the six days of creation it is said: 'And God saw that it was good' (*Genesis 1:10*). As is stated in the Catechism of the Catholic Church: 'By the very nature of creation, material being is endowed with its own stability, truth and excellence, its own order and laws. Each of the various creatures, willed in its own being, reflects in its own way a ray of God's infinite wisdom and goodness.'"[16] All the animals in creation, as suggested by *The Call of Creation* and promoted in the catechism, are willed for their own sake, exist because God has decided

---

13. CBCEW, *Call of Creation*, 7–10.
14. CBCEW, *Call of Creation*, 7–10.
15. John Paul II, *Redemptor Hominis*, §15.
16. CBCEW, *Call of Creation*, 15–18.

that they should and, by their existence, reflect the infinite wisdom and goodness of God himself.

These significant avenues in thinking show something of a development from earlier teaching. In the same chapter, we read, "While our destructiveness can silence creation's song of praise to God, our care for creation can be a true expression of our own praise. Such perspectives challenge narrow and materialistic and utilitarian views that the gifts of creation only have value as a 'factor of production.'"[17] This seems to me to be saying that the earth, in all its creative diversity, in existing to praise God, can be silenced by human destructiveness and neglect; that each animal, as part of that creation, should be treated with care and compassion as a gift from God; that animals are not "factor[s] of production," but divinely-willed, even breath-spirit-filled creatures, whose existence gives praise to God and who lead us to further discover our own call to praise him.

In this most recent of documents, the church is moving towards a greater focus on the environment and, indeed, on the place of animals within that context. Creation, and all of the earth's creatures, are seen as ends in themselves, not things which are primarily for the use of human beings. Whilst, unsurprisingly, the document naturally testifies to the place of the unique and divinely ordered human being within creation, it also calls for humans to act with more compassion and sensitivity to the planet on which we live and, indeed, to the beings with which we share the planet, not least because of the human reality of being made in the image of God.

It should also be recognised that the church is so much more than her official teaching and documents—or even, indeed, the popes and the bishops. It is the lay men and women who are the largest praying, worshipping, and active community within the body of Christ. Deborah M. Jones, following her doctoral research, points out some interesting results after a group of Roman Catholics were asked to comment on the animal-related paragraphs in the catechism.[18] She reveals that "none of the interviewees displayed knowledge of any church teaching about animals and their welfare. None had ever heard a homily on the subject, or given one, although most had heard of animal blessing services."[19] She says, further, that "evidence was shown of gender differences in approach to the issue of animals—the women being generally the more sympathetic towards animals,

---

17. CBCEW, *Call of Creation*, 7–10.
18. Jones, "Can There Be."
19. Jones, *Compassion*, 203.

and the men, particularly the celibate clergy, less so, even—in some cases—hostile," a challenging observation but one that is borne out by this author's experience.[20] Jones finally notes, insightfully, that "with lives totally ordered to ministry towards people . . . there would be only wonder why a priest in today's Church should be sympathetic to animals."[21]

One commentator recounts an occasion, when asked to provide a presentation on animals and the Catholic Church to a group of Catholic bishops, where a palpable degree of resistance was encountered—as if genuine concern for animals precluded genuine consideration for people (which, of course, need not be, and generally is not, the case). It was only at conclusion of formal business, in the relative quiet of face-to-face conversation, that individual bishops felt able to declare their interest in animals, rather than publicly at the meeting. There is still a sense, somehow, that caring for animals and expressing a genuine concern for their well-being under God is less than completely Catholic or Christian. It must be possible, surely, to both celebrate the fullness of one's own faith as a practising Catholic Christian and, at the same time, to hold serious beliefs about animals and their care. Kindness and concern for animals does not compromise Catholicism! In the walking together that the synodal path of Pope Francis offers to the church, it may be that the voice of the laity advocating for animals will be stronger than that of the clergy. The inevitable question, if and when lay Catholics do speak up and call for a genuine Christian concern for animals, must wonder whether they will be heard.

There is still something of a journey to be made, but the church is gradually, I suggest, moving towards the reality of animals being seen for who they are: inhabitants with us of the planet which the creator has freely and lovingly given, deserving of notice because they exist by divine ordinance; sentient, God-created beings who are ends in themselves: beautiful, mysterious, godly, and essential for the health and well-being of the planet and of the whole human race.

Laudato Si', Pope Francis

> Our insistence that each human being is an image of God should not make us overlook the fact that each creature has its own

---

20. Jones, *Compassion*, 219.
21. Jones, *Compassion*, 226.

purpose. None is superfluous. The entire material universe speaks of God's love, his boundless affection for us.[22]

Prayer

Christ Jesus, you are the beginning and the end.
In you all things were created and in you all things are redeemed.
Christ Jesus, you are Lord of creation.
It was for all that you gave your life on the cross, a perfect sacrifice.
Take now, to your open arms, our grief for your creation:
for your wildlife, struggling against extinction;
for the hunted and the trapped;
for the abandoned and the homeless;
for your food animals, unnaturally imprisoned, transported and slaughtered in terror;
for your animals cruelly used as laboratory tools.
Christ Jesus, in us you live as Risen Lord.
Our hearts plead with you now to carry the pain of your suffering creatures, even to the least of these.
The darkness of the world binds them as it binds us, O Lord,
and only your love can free us to live in your light.
Christ Jesus, come, redeem your world.
In your holy name we pray, Amen.

(May Tripp)[23]

---

22. Francis, *LS*, §84.
23. Cited in Linzey and Regan, *Compassion*, 89–90.

Conclusion

An Animal Friendly Church?

*I will make for them a covenant on that day with
the beasts of the field, the birds of the heavens,
and the creeping things of the ground.*

(Hosea 2:18)

*Fear not, you beasts of the field, for the pastures
of the wilderness are green.*

(Joel 2:22)

I REMEMBER, WHEN I was newly ordained, preparing for a funeral at the crematorium. It may well have been my very first. I had arrived early in order to compose myself. As time pressed on, I realised that we were due to begin the funeral at any moment but that as yet no coffin or mourners had appeared. I began to feel worried and unsettled. I spoke to a member of the crematorium staff, who was no doubt somewhat more experienced and worldly wise than me and shared my concern. "Oh, don't worry," he said confidently, "we can start without them."

"Great," said I, "let's get on with it then," before realising what a foolish thing I had said. The staff member was full of laughter and kindness but had clearly thoroughly enjoyed teasing this new boy who still had so much to learn.

I still have a great deal to learn. My understanding of animals and their place in God's plan for the world has developed gradually but insistently. I regret that it has taken me so many years to actually open my eyes to the wonder of who animals are and what God is doing when he creates them. *Mea culpa.*

On the advice of a friend whose opinion I greatly value, I decided some years ago to provide the opportunity for confessions on a daily basis in the parish. Some claim that this sacrament is a little neglected these days, and I wanted to help my parishioners to see what a wonderful and life-changing gift is the Sacrament of Reconciliation. On arrival in the parish, from the first Sunday of my time there, I announced that confessions would be available every day. Then I prepared myself to be disappointed. I expected to spend hours each week waiting for the people to come and finding that my passion for this particular gift was misplaced and even, perhaps, foolish. I need not have worried. The good people of the parish started to come, they kept coming, and still they come. Good habits appear to lead to the proliferation of more good habits. Throughout the deanery and beyond, folk know that the sacrament is very available in the parish and, as a result, they will travel some distance to find solace from God in this particular way. Often, folk will tug at my arm and request whether I can make time for a "quick confession." It is a beautiful thing when we see God's grace and mercy at work and, for the priest especially, a marvellous privilege to minister in this way. It is, perhaps, very many years indeed since confessions were so freely available in the parish.

I mention this because, through it, I have learned that it is possible to change habits and to establish new customs. In a Christian understanding of the world, leopards really can change their spots. God's good people are remarkably adept at finding new ways (or of rediscovering old ways) to connect with him and of allowing/inviting him to connect with them. I admit to being thrilled at the emphasis which is given to confessions in the parish, and to the defining part which that custom plays in people's understanding of how we tick as celebrating Catholics in that place. To go to confession is to accept a little revolution within our own hearts; it is to understand that God can renew everything about who we are and provide us with the freedom which we need to see more clearly. Truly, habits can change, and minds can be reset. It is an example of what radical power God has to shift our perspective and to afford us a brand-new beginning.

This little book has turned out to be a much greater undertaking than I had imagined. My hope is that it has been helpful. As I wrote it, I always had in mind my current parishioners, since I want the text and the sentiments, the questions and the challenges, to speak especially to them. Thus, I have rooted this manuscript in the thing which I know best, my ministry as a Catholic priest. The anecdotes are all true, although names have been changed. Each event which I describe is simply a recalling of many pastoral encounters through the years. If it is helpful for Christians of all denominations and, indeed, to any who are seeking some broader sense of correlation between the world and faith, then thanks be to God.

I pray that the ideas and thoughts communicated here will help the reader to consider the place of all animals in their own life, and to deepen their already existing desire to see animals always treated with kindness and compassion. The choices which you make are for you, but if this book has helped to inform your conscience in making those choices, or has assisted you in raising up new questions, or has challenged previously held perceptions and considerations, then this little offering will have been worthwhile.

Further, I have a wild hope that this very personal and anecdotal contribution to the debate around the place of animals within Catholicism/Christianity, will make some small difference and even, dare I consider it, spur on Catholic thinking in this area. We have seen that theology and pastoral considerations around animals *are* gradually changing and developing, even in the vast, slow-moving family which is the Catholic Church.

The conversations around animals (for people of faith and for those of none) need to change. I believe passionately in all that I have written here, as is probably self-evident. We can no longer treat animals as mere playthings, or thoughtlessly as sources of food, or as objects of human entertainment and work. It seems to me that God desires and deserves that animals be given the care and compassion which are rightly theirs as part of his glorious creation. Writing the foreword to Dom Ambrose Agius's *God's Animals* in 1970, John Cardinal Heenan, Archbishop of Westminster, said that "[animals] have positive rights because they are God's creatures. If we have to speak with absolute accuracy we must say that *God has the right to have all his creatures treated with proper respect*."[1] That says it all, really.

---

1. Agius, *God's Animals*, 3; my emphasis.

An Animal Friendly Church?

Perhaps, with the short reflections that I have presented here, minds can be changed, and hearts stirred.

Please do remember that if you're an animal-loving Catholic or Christian who has been helped by what you have read, there is encouragement and support for you out there. The small charity Catholic Concern for Animals, which will joyously celebrate its centenary in 2029, is an excellent place to start, and other Christian support groups and interest groups can easily be found online. Specifically, speaking out for animals within the church can leave us feeling isolated and alone, such is the status quo. Those of us for whom these matters raise genuine concern need to find, and to celebrate, fruitful mutual support and friendship.

It will be clear to the reader that I have worn my heart on my sleeve. I certainly care intensely about all the animals whom God has given to us, and with whom we are called to share the planet. I make no apology for such concern because, in the words of Jesus himself, I can declare, "For where [my] treasure is, there will [my] heart be also" (Matt 6:21). Within the context of my cherished Catholic faith and of my desire to follow Jesus, the animals are the treasure in whom I have placed my heart—and they have given back (and continue to give back) so much more than I could ever have hoped or imagined. In the name of the Lord and of the church, I owe and dedicate this offering to them and resolve that, wherever it is within my power, I will never cooperate with the material means which cause them suffering or to be exploited.

Pope St. John Paul II urged human beings to always collaborate with God and with God's creation, for it is dangerous not to: "Instead of carrying out his role as a cooperator with God in the work of creation, man sets himself up in place of God and thus ends up provoking a rebellion on the part of nature, which is more tyrannised than governed by him. . . . In all this, one notes first the poverty or narrowness of man's outlook, motivated as he is by a desire to possess things rather than to relate them to the truth, and lacking that disinterested, unselfish and aesthetic attitude that is born of wonder in the presence of being and of the beauty which enables one to see in visible things the message of the invisible God who created them."[2]

St. Bonaventure, biographer of St. Francis, sees Jesus in all created things:

> Every creature is a divine word, because by God they are proclaimed . . .

---

2. John Paul II, *Centessimus Annus*, §37.

> Christ has something in common with all creatures.
> With the stone he shares existence,
> with the plants he shares life,
> with the animals he shares sensation
> and with the angels he shares intelligence.
> Thus all things are transformed in Christ
> since in the fullness of his nature,
> he embraces some part of every creature.[3]

The great priest-theologian and doctor of the church, St. John of Avila, writes beautifully when he says, "Turn your eyes to this whole world, which was created for your sake alone, together with all the creatures it contains: this too signifies love, proclaims love, and shares love with you."[4]

Please God, readers will discover here some encouragement to reflect again, or even to start anew: to love God's little ones, the animals, and to honour the part that all creatures play in God's extraordinary and profound creation.

---

3. Hayes, *Christ, Word of God*, 13.
4. John of Avila, "Divine Office," 1.2.4.

Bibliography

Abbate, Cheryl. "Non-Human Animals; Not Necessarily Saints or Sinners." *Between the Species* 17.1 (2014) article 1. DOI: https://doi.org/10.15368/bts.2014v17n1.4.

Adam, Margaret. "Why Should Christians Care about Animals?" SARX: For All God's Creatures, 2017. https://sarx.org.uk/articles/christianity-and-animals/why-should-christians-care-about-animals/.

Agius, A. *God's Animals*. London: Catholic Study Circle for Animal Welfare, 1970.

———. "Why Cruelty Is a Sin to Animals (1960)." *The Ark*, 90th anniversary ed., 243 (Autumn 2019).

Anderson, Kip, and Kameron Waters. *Christpiracy*. AUM Films and Media, 2024.

Aquinas, Thomas. *Of God and His Creatures of the Summa Contra Gentiles*. Translated by Joseph Rickaby. N.p.: The Catholic Primer, 2005. https://basilica.ca/documents/2016/10/St.%20Thomas%20Aquinas-The%20Summa%20Contra%20Gentiles.pdf.

———. *Summa Theologiae*. Notre Dame, IN: Ave Maria, 2000.

Arluke, A., and C. R. Sanders. *Regarding Animals*. Philadelphia: Temple University Press, 1996.

Armstrong, Susan J., and R. G. Botzler, eds. *The Animal Ethics Reader*. 2nd ed. London: Routledge, 2008.

Aseneta, Anatoly A. R. "Laudato Si' on Non-Human Animals." *Journal of Moral Theology* 6.2 (2017) 230–45.

Athanasius. *Contra Gentes*. Oxford: Clarendon, 1971.

———. *Letter to Serapion on the Holy Spirit*. Translated by C. Shapland. London: Epworth, 1951.

Augustine. *City of God*. London: Penguin, 2003.

Baggini, J. *The Pig That Wants to Be Eaten*. New York: Penguin, 2005.

Barad, J. A. *Aquinas on the Nature and Treatment of Animals*. San Francisco: International Scholars, 1995.

Barbour, Hugh. "Why the Church Blesses Animals." Catholic Answers, 2023. https://www.catholic.com/magazine/online-edition/why-the-church-blesses-animals.

Barth, Karl. *Church Dogmatics*. Edinburgh: T&T Clark, 1978.

Beauchamp, T. L., and R. G. Frey, eds. *The Oxford Handbook of Animal Ethics*. New York: Oxford University Press, 2011.

Bede. *The Age of Bede*. Rev. ed. London: Penguin Classics, 1998.

Bekoff, M. *The Emotional Lives of Animals: A Leading Scientist Explores Animal Joy*. California: New World Library, 2007.

Bibliography

Bekoff, M., and C. A. Meaney, eds. *Encyclopaedia of Animal Rights and Animal Welfare.* Westport, CT: Greenwood, 1998.

Bekoff, M., and J. Pierce. *The Animals' Agenda.* Boston: Beacon, 2017.

Benedict XVI. *Caritas in Veritate.* London: Catholic Truth Society, 2009.

———. *The Garden of God: Toward a Human Ecology.* Washington: Catholic University America Press, 2014.

———. "General Audience." The Holy See, Jan. 27, 2010. https://www.vatican.va/content/benedict-xvi/en/audiences/2010/documents/hf_ben-xvi_aud_20100127.html.

———. "Homily of His Holiness Benedict XVI: Celebration of Vespers with the Faithful." The Holy See, July 24, 2009. https://www.vatican.va/content/benedict-xvi/en/homilies/2009/documents/hf_ben-xvi_hom_20090724_vespri-aosta.html.

———. "World Day of Peace: If You Want to Cultivate Peace, Protect Creation." The Holy See, Jan. 1, 2010. https://www.vatican.va/content/benedict-xvi/en/messages/peace/documents/hf_ben-xvi_mes_20091208_xliii-world-day-peace.html.

———. "World Day of Peace: Educating Young People in Justice and Peace." The Holy See, Jan. 1, 2012. https://www.vatican.va/content/benedict-xvi/en/messages/peace/documents/hf_ben-xvi_mes_20111208_xlv-world-day-peace.html.

Bentham, Jeremy. *An Introduction to the Principles of Morals and Legislation.* Edited by J. H. Burns and H. L. A Hart. Oxford: Clarendon, 1996.

Berkman, John. "All of Creation Glorifies God." SARX: For All God's Creatures, n.d. Video interview, 11:35. https://sarx.org.uk/multimedia/filmed-interviews/john-berkman/.

———. "Are We Addicted to the Suffering Of Animals? Animal Cruelty and the Catholic Moral Tradition." In *A Faith Embracing All Creatures: Addressing Commonly Asked Questions about Christian Care for Animals*, edited by Tripp York and Andy Alexis-Baker, 124–37. Eugene, OR: Cascade, 2012.

———. "Are We All Michael Vick?" Catholic Moral Theology, 2011. https://catholicmoraltheology.com/are-we-all-michael-vick-our-addiction-to-animal-cruelty-a-call-to-conversion/.

———. "The Consumption of Animals and the Catholic Tradition." *Logos—Journal of Catholic Thought and Culture* 7.1 (Winter 2004) 174–90. https://www.academia.edu/3256484/The_Consumption_of_Animals_and_the_Catholic_Tradition_2004_?f_ri=97020.

———. "From Theological Speciesism to a Theological Ethology: Where Catholic Moral Theology Needs to Go." *Journal of Moral Theology* 3.2 (2014) 11–34. https://jmt.scholasticahq.com/article/11265-from-theologial-speciesism-to-a-theological-ethology-where-catholic-moral-theology-needs-to-go.

———. "Homily for the Feast of St. Francis." Catholic Moral Theology, Sept. 25, 2011. https://catholicmoraltheology.com/homily-for-feast-of-st-francis-blessing-of-animals-service/.

———. "Just Chimpanzees? A Thomistic Perspective on Ethics in a Non-Human Species." In *Beastly Morality: Animals as Ethical Agents*, edited by Jonathan K. Crane, 195–224. New York: Columbia University Press, 2015.

———. "Medicine, Animals and Theology." *St. Mark's Review* 149 (1992) 32–36.

———. "Must We Love Non-Human Beings?" *New Blackfriars* 102.1099 (2021) 322–38.

———. "Prophetically Pro-Life: John Paul II's Gospel of Life and Evangelical Concern for Animals." *Josephinum Journal of Theology* 6.1 (1999) 56.

Bibliography

———. "A Theology of Animal Happiness." SARX: For All God's Creatures, 2018. Video lecture, 17:13. https://sarx.org.uk/multimedia/creature-conference-talks/a-theology-animal-happiness/.

———. "Towards a Thomistic Theology of Animality." In *Creaturely Theology*, edited by Celia Deane-Drummond and David Clough, 21–40. London: SCM, 2009. https://www.academia.edu/3183357/Towards_a_Thomistic_Theology_of_Animality_2009_.

"Blessing of the Animals." St Joseph Catholic Church, n.d. https://www.sjccc.net/blessing_of_the_animals.

Bonaventure. *The Life of St. Francis of Assisi*. Gastonia, NC: TAN Classics, 2010.

Bouyer, Louis. *Eucharist*. Notre Dame: University of Notre Dame Press, 1968.

Butler, Alban. *Butler's Lives of the Saints*. Vol. 2. London: Continuum, 1998.

Camosy, Charles. *For Love of Animals: Christian Ethics, Consistent Action*. Cincinnati: Franciscan Media, 2013.

———. "God's Plan for Animals Is a Hot Topic in Theology That We Can All Understand." *National Catholic Reporter*, May 6, 2021. https://www.ncronline.org/earthbeat/faith/gods-plan-animals-hot-topic-theology-we-can-all-understand.

———. *Peter Singer and Christian Ethics*. Cambridge: Cambridge University Press, 2012.

———. "Pope's Eco-Encyclical a Breakthrough in Thinking about Animals." Interview with John Berkman. Crux, Jun. 18, 2016. https://cruxnow.com/interviews/2016/06/popes-eco-encyclical-breakthrough-thinking-animals.

Catechism of the Catholic Church. London: Geoffrey Chapman, 1994.

Catherine of Siena. *The Dialogue of St. Catherine*. North Carolina: TAN Books, 1991.

Catholic Concern for Animals. "Prayers." n.d. https://catholic-animals.com/prayers/.

Catholic Rural Life. "October—Blessing of Animals." n.d. https://catholicrurallife.org/resources/spiritual/calendar-of-blessings/10-october-blessing-of-animals/.

Cavalieri, Paolo. *The Animal Question*. Oxford: Oxford University Press, 2004.

Cavalieri, Paolo, and Peter Singer. *The Great Ape Project: Equality beyond Humanity*. New York: St. Martin's, 1993.

CBCEW. *The Call of Creation*. London: CBCEW, 2022.

CCCC. London: Catholic Truth Society, 2006.

Chardin, Pierre Teilhard de. *Hymn of the Universe*. New York: Harper & Row, 1961.

Clark, S. R. L. *The Moral Status of Animals*. Oxford: Clarendon, 1977.

Clough David L. "Animals: Who Cares?" SARX: For All God's Creatures, n.d. https://sarx.org.uk/articles/christianity-and-animals/animals-who-cares/.

———. *On Animals: Systematic Theology*. London: Bloomsbury, 2013.

———. *On Animals: Theological Ethics*. London: Bloomsbury, 2019.

———. "The Challenge of Christian Animal Ethics: An Interview with David Clough." Interface, 2018. https://regentinterface.com/resource/the-challenge-of-christian-animal-ethics-an-interview-with-david-clough/.

Cochrane, A. *Animal Rights without Liberation: Applied Ethics and Human Obligation*. New York: Columbia University Press, 2012.

Covey, Allison. "With Every Living Creature That Is with You: Exploring Relational Ontology and Non-Human Animals." PhD diss., University of St. Michael's College, 2020. https://tspace.library.utoronto.ca/bitstream/1807/104781/5/Covey_Allison_M_202011_PhD_thesis.pdf.

"A CreatureKind Lectionary for All Creation: For Animals, Peoples and the Earth." CreatureKind, n.d. https://www.becreaturekind.org/the-creaturekind-lectionary.

Bibliography

Davis, K. *Prisoned Chickens, Poisoned Eggs*. 2nd ed. Summertown, TN: Book Publishing Company, 2009.

Deane-Drummond, Celia. "Are Animals Moral? A Theological Appraisal of the Evolution of Vice and Virtue." *Zygon* 44.4 (Dec. 2009) 933–49. https://www.academia.edu/17873055/ARE_ANIMALS_MORAL_A_THEOLOGICAL_APPRAISAL_OF_THE_EVOLUTION_OF_VICE_AND_VIRTUE.

———. *Re-Imaging the Divine Image: Humans and Other Animals*. Kitchener, ON: Pandora, 2014.

Deane-Drummond, Celia, and David Clough, eds. *Creaturely Theology*. London: SCM, 2009.

Deane-Drummond, Celia, et al., eds. *Animals as Religious Subjects*. London: Bloomsbury, 2013.

DeGrazia, D. *Animal Rights*. Oxford: Oxford University Press, 2002.

———. *Taking Animals Seriously*. New York: Cambridge University Press, 1996.

Descartes, Rene. *Discourse on Method and The Meditations*. London: Penguin 2005.

———. "Meditations 1 and 2." Chad Vance, n.d. https://rintintin.colorado.edu/~vancecd/phil201/Meditations.pdf.

Dhont, K., and G. Hodson. *Why We Love and Exploit Animals*. London: Routledge, 2020.

Donaldson, S., and W. Kymlicka. *Zoopolis; A Political Theory of Animal Rights*. Oxford: Oxford University Press, 2011.

Dorcy, M. J. *St. Dominic's Family*. North Carolina: TAN Books, 1983.

Dostoyevsky, Fyodor. *The Brothers Karamazov*. London: Penguin Classics, 2003.

Druce, C., and Philip Lymbery. *Outlawed in Europe: How America Is Falling behind Europe in Farm Animal Welfare*. Woodbury, CT: Archimedian, 2002.

D'Silva, Joyce. *Animal Welfare in World Religion: Teaching and Practice*. London: Routledge, 2023.

Dunayer, J. *Animal Equality: Language and Liberation*. Maryland: Ryce, 2001.

Eadmer. *The Life of St. Anselm*. Edited by R. W. Southern. Oxford: Oxford University Press, 2012.

Eisnitz, G. A. *Slaughterhouse*. Lanham, MD: Prometheus, 2007.

Elvins, Mark. "St. Francis, Creation and Original Innocence." *The Ark*, 90th anniversary ed., 243 (Autumn 2019).

Fiddes, N. *Meat: A Natural Symbol*. London: Routledge, 1991.

Foer, Jonathan Safran. *Eating Animals*. New York: Little Brown, 2009.

Fortini, Arnaldo. *Francis of Assisi*. Translated by Helen Moak. New York: Crossroad, 1980.

Francione, Gary L. *Animals as Persons: Essays on the Abolition of Animal Exploitation*. New York: Columbia University Press, 2008.

———. *Introduction to Animal Rights: Your Child or the Dog*. Philadelphia: Temple University Press, 2000.

Francione, Gary L., and A. Charlton. *Advocate for Animals!* London: Exempla, 2017.

———. *Animal Rights*. London: Exempla, 2015.

———. *Eat Like You Care: An Examination of the Morals of Eating Animals*. London: Exempla, 2013.

Francis. "General Audience." The Holy See, May 1, 2013. https://www.vatican.va/content/francesco/en/audiences/2013/documents/papa-francesco_20130501_udienza-generale.html.

———. *Laudate Deum*. The Holy See, 2023. https://www.vatican.va/content/francesco/en/apost_exhortations/documents/20231004-laudate-deum.html.

Bibliography

———. *Laudato Si', On Care for our Common Home*. London: Catholic Truth Society, 2015.

———. *Lumen Fidei*. London: Catholic Truth Society, 2013.

———. "Mass, Imposition of the Pallium and Bestowal of the Fisherman's Ring for the Beginning of the Petrine Ministry of the Bishop of Rome." The Holy See, Mar. 19, 2013. https://www.vatican.va/content/francesco/en/homilies/2013/documents/papa-francesco_20130319_omelia-inizio-pontificato.html.

Francis of Assisi. "Canticle of the Creatures." Jesuitresource.org, n.d. https://www.xavier.edu/jesuitresource/online-resources/prayer-index/creation-prayers.

Free, Ann Cottrell. *Animals, Nature and Albert Schweitzer*. Washington, DC: The Humane Society of the United States, 1982.

Gaspari, Pietro. "Creation Is Disposed to Perfection." *The Ark* (Aug. 1953).

Godlovitch, S., et al., eds. *Animals, Men and Morals: An Enquiry into the Maltreatment of Non-Humans*. London: Victor Gollancz, 1971.

Graves, Robert. "In the Wilderness." All Poetry, n.d. https://allpoetry.com/In-The-Wilderness.

Greek, R., and N Shanks. *FAQs about the Use of Animals in Science*. Maryland: University Press of America, 2009.

Gruen, L. *Ethics and Animals: An Introduction*. Cambridge: Cambridge University Press, 2011.

Hayes, Zachary. "Christ, Word of God and Exemplar of Humanity." *The Cord* 46.1 (1996) 1–4.

Heaster, Duncan. "Legion and the Gadarene Pigs." https://www.academia.edu/5722896/Legion_and_the_Gadarene_Pigs.

Henig, Martin. "Christianity and the Rights of Animals by Andrew Linzey (Review)." *Journal of Animal Ethics* 10.1 (Spring 2020) 82–84. https://muse.jhu.edu/pub/34/article/754247/pdf.

Hobgood-Oster, L. *The Friends We Keep: Unleashing Christianity's Compassion for Animals*. London: Darton Longman & Todd, 2010.

Hofler, Anthony. "Is Eternal Life for Humans Only?" *The Ark*, Summer 2023.

Horrell, D. G. *The Bible and the Environment: Towards a Critical Ecological Biblical Theology*. London: Equinox, 2010.

International Theological Commission. *Communion and Stewardship: Human Persons Created in the Image of God*. The Holy See, 2004. https://www.vatican.va/roman_curia/congregations/cfaith/cti_documents/rc_con_cfaith_doc_20040723_communion-stewardship_en.html.

Jandu, J. P. *The Garden of Vegan*. Xplore!, 2017.

John of Avila. "Divine Office, Office of Readings, Second Reading (For the Newly Established Memorial in 2021): *Tractatus de amore Dei erga nos*." Madrid: n.p., 2004.

John of the Cross. *Collected Works*. Washington, DC: ICS, 1991.

John Paul II. "Al Popolo di Assisi [To the People of Assisi]." The Holy See, Mar. 12, 1982. https://www.vatican.va/content/john-paul-ii/it/speeches/1982/march/documents/hf_jp-ii_spe_19820312_popolo-assisi.html.

———. *Centessimus Annus*. The Holy See, 1991. https://www.vatican.va/content/john-paul-ii/en/encyclicals/documents/hf_jp-ii_enc_04031979_redemptor-hominis.html.

———. *Evangelium Vitae*. London: Catholic Truth Society, 1995.

Bibliography

———. "Letter to Artists." The Holy See, 1999. https://www.vatican.va/content/john-paul-ii/en/letters/1999/documents/hf_jp-ii_let_23041999_artists.html.
———. *Redemptor Hominis*. London: Catholic Truth Society, 1979.
———. *Sollicitudo Rei Socialis*. London: Catholic Truth Society, 1988.
———. "Udienza Generale." The Holy See, Jan. 10, 1990. Translated by Bryan Jerabek. https://www.vatican.va/content/john-paul-ii/it/audiences/1990/documents/hf_jp-ii_aud_19900110.html.
Johnson, L. *Power, Knowledge, Animals*. London: Palgrave Macmillan, 2012.
Jones, Deborah M. "Can There Be a Roman Catholic Theology of Animals?" PhD diss., University of Wales, Lampeter, 2008.
———. *The School of Compassion: A Roman Catholic Theology of Animals*. Leominster: Gracewing, 2009.
Joy, M. *Strategic Action for Animals*. New York: Lantern, 2008.
Julian of Norwich. *Revelations of Divine Love*. London: Penguin, 1998.
Kao, Grace Y. "Creaturely Solidarity: Rethinking Human-Nonhuman Animal Relations." *Journal of Religious Ethics* 42.4 (2014) 743–68. https://www.academia.edu/9607497/_Creaturely_Solidarity_Rethinking_Human_Nonhuman_Animal_Relations_2014_.
Kaufman, S. R., and N. Braun. *Good News for All Creation*. Cleveland: Vegetarian Advocates, 2004.
Kempis, Thomas à. *The Imitation of Christ*. London: Penguin, 1973.
Kowalski, G. *The Souls of Animals*. New Hampshire: Stillpoint, 1991.
Laudate Hymn Book. Suffolk: Decani Music/Books, 2012.
Linzey, Andrew. *Animal Gospel*. Louisville: Westminster John Knox, 2000.
———. *Animal Rites: Liturgies of Animal Care*. London: SCM, 1999.
———. *Creatures of the Same God: Explorations in Animal Theology*. Winchester: Winchester University Press, 2007.
———. *Dictionary of Ethics, Theology and Society*. London: Routledge, 1996.
———. *An Ethical Critique of Fur Factory Farming*. London: Palgrave Macmillan, 2020.
———. *Ethical Vegetarianism and Veganism*. London: Routledge, 2018.
———, ed. *The Global Guide to Animal Protection*. Urbana, IL: University of Illinois Press, 2013.
———, ed. *The Link between Animal Abuse and Human Violence*. Brighton: Sussex Academic, 2009.
———. "The Neglected Creature: The Doctrine of Non-Human Creation and Its Relationship with the Human in the Thought of Karl Barth." PhD thesis, King's College, 1986. https://kclpure.kcl.ac.uk/portal/en/studentTheses/the-neglected-creature-the-doctrine-of-the-non-human-creation-and.
———. *Why Animal Suffering Matters*. Oxford: Oxford University Press, 2009.
Linzey Andrew, and Clair Linzey, eds. *Animal Ethics and Animal Law*. Lanham, MD: Lexington, 2011.
———. *Animal Theologians*. Oxford: Oxford University Press, 2023.
———. *Animal Theology*. Chicago: University of Illinois Press, 1995.
———. *Christianity and the Rights of Animals*. London: SPCK, 1987.
———, eds. *The Palgrave Handbook of Practical Animal Ethics*. London: Palgrave Macmillan, 2018.
———, eds. *The Routledge Handbook of Religion and Animal Ethics*. London: Routledge, 2020.
Linzey, Andrew, and D. Cohn-Sherbok. *After Noah*. London: Mowbray, 1997.

Linzey, Andrew, and Dorothy Yamamoto, eds. *Animals on the Agenda*. London: SCM, 1998.
Linzey, Andrew, and P. B. Clarke, eds. *Animal Rights: A Historical Anthology*. New York: Columbia University Press, 1990.
Linzey, Andrew, and Tom Regan, eds. *Animals and Christianity*. London: SPCK, 1989.
———, eds. *Compassion for Animals: Readings and Prayers*. London: SPCK, 1988.
———, eds. *The Ethical Case against Animal Experiments*. Urbana, IL: University of Illinois Press, 2018.
———, eds. *Other Nations: Animals in Modern Literature*. Waco, TX: Baylor University Press, 2010.
Linzey, Clair. "Animals in Catholic Thought: A New Sensitivity." *Dialogue and Universalism* 24.1 (2014) 141–55.
———. *Developing Animal Theology: An Engagement with Leonardo Boff*. London: Routledge, 2022.
Lossky, Vladimir. *The Mystical Theology of the Eastern Church*. Cambridge: James Clark, 1957.
Loughnan, Steven. "The Psychology of Eating Animals." *Current Directions in Psychological Science* 23.2 (2015) 104–8.
Lurz, R. W. ed. *The Philosophy of Animal Minds*. Cambridge: Cambridge University Press, 1991.
Lymbery, Philip, and I. Oakeshott. *Farmageddon: The True Cost of Cheap Meat*. London: Bloomsbury, 2014.
Masson, J. *The Pig Who Sang to the Moon*. London: Vintage, 2005.
Maurice, F. D. *Sermons Preached in Country Churches*. London: Macmillan, 1880.
McLaughlin, R. P. *Christian Theology and the Status of Animals*. Basingstoke, England: Palgrave Macmillan, 2014.
Meyer, Eric D. "They Fell Silent When We Stopped Listening: Apophatic Theology and 'Asking the Beasts.'" In *Turning to the Heavens and the Earth: Theological Reflections on a Cosmological Conversion; Essays in Honor of Elizabeth A. Johnson*, edited by Julia Brumbaugh and Natalie Imperatori-Lee, 26–44. Collegeville, MN: Liturgical, 2016.
Miller, Michael J., trans. *YouCat: Youth Catechism of the Catholic Church*. San Francisco: Ignatius, 2011.
Miller, R. J. *The Rise and Fall of Animal Experimentation*. Oxford: Oxford University Press, 2023.
More, Thomas. *Utopia*. London: Penguin, 2012.
Morrison, A. R. *An Odyssey with Animals: A Veterinarian's Reflection on the Animal Rights and Welfare Debate*. New York: Oxford University Press, 2009.
Murray, R. *The Cosmic Covenant*. London: Continuum International, 1992.
Newkirk, I. *Free the Animals*. New York: Lantern, 2000.
Newman, J. H. *The Crucifixion, Parochial and Plain Sermons*. 8 vols. London: Rivingtons, 1888.
Nibert, D. A. *Animal Oppression and Human Violence*. New York: Columbia University Press, 2013.
———. *Animal Rights/Human Rights: Entanglements of Oppression and Liberation*. New York: Rowman & Littlefield, 2002.
Noske, B. *Beyond Boundaries: Humans and Animals*. Montreal: Black Rose, 1997.

Bibliography

OneKind. "OneKind Talks Animal Ethics with Andrew Linzey." June 21, 2011. https://onekind.scot.archived.website/onekindblog/article/onekind_talks_animal_ethics_with_andrew_linzey.html.

Order of Confirmation, Catholic Truth Society, London, 2016.

The Orthodox Fellowship of the Transfiguration. "St. Seraphim of Sarov (1759–1833)." N.d. https://www.orth-transfiguration.org/resources/library/writings-of-the-saints/st-seraphim-sarov-1759-1833/.

Pacifici, Mimmo. "The Pope Has Said: Animals Too Have Souls, Just Like Men." Dream Shore, Jan. 1990. https://www.dreamshore.net/rococo/pope.html.

Paterson, D., and Richard Ryder, eds. *Animals' Rights—A Symposium*. Sussex: Centaur, 1979.

Patterson, C. *Eternal Treblinka: Our Treatment of Animals and the Holocaust*. New York: Lantern, 2021.

Paul VI. *Humanae Vitae*. London: Catholic Truth Society, 2008.

"Peace Prayer." Loyola Press, n.d. https://www.loyolapress.com/catholic-resources/prayer/traditional-catholic-prayers/saints-prayers/peace-prayer-of-saint-francis/.

Phelps, N. *The Dominion of Love: Animals Rights according to the Bible*. New York: Lantern, 2002.

Pius V. *Bulla super prohibitione agitationis taurorum et ferarum, et annullatione votorum et iuramentorum, super eisdem pro tempore interpositorum [De Salute Gregis Dominici]*. Rome: Vatican, 1567.

Pius XI. *Casti Conubii*. Encyclical, the Holy See, Dec. 31, 1930. https://www.vatican.va/content/pius-xi/en/encyclicals/documents/hf_p-xi_enc_19301231_casti-connubii.html

———. *Rite Expiatis on St Francis of Assisi*. Washington: National Catholic Welfare Conference, 1926.

Pius XII. "The Structure of the Matter of the Created World as a Manifestation of the Wisdom and Goodness of God: Address to the Pontifical Academy of Sciences." Apr. 24, 1955. https://www.pas.va/en/magisterium/servant-of-god-pius-xii/1955-24-april.html.

Pontifical Work for Ecclesiastical Vocations. *New Vocations for a New Europe*. The Holy See, Jan. 6, 1998. https://www.vatican.va/roman_curia/congregations/ccatheduc/documents/rc_con_ccatheduc_doc_13021998_new-vocations_en.html.

Poorva, Joshipura. *Survival at Stake*. New York: HarperCollins, 2023.

"Prayers and Liturgies for Animals." St. Margaret's Episcopal Church, n.d. http://www.stmargaretschurch.org/worship/prayers-and-liturgies-for-animals.html.

"Prayers for Animals/Creation." Pan-Orthodox Concern for Animals, n.d. http://panorthodoxconcernforanimals.org/prayers-for-creation/.

Primatt, Humphrey. *Dissertation on the Duty of Mercy and Sin of Cruelty to Brute Animals*. Edinburgh: Constable, 1834.

Ratzinger, Joseph. *God and the World: A Conversation with Peter Seewald*. San Francisco: Ignatius, 2002.

———. *The Spirit of the Liturgy*. San Francisco: Ignatius, 2000.

Regan, Tom. *The Case for Animal Rights*. Berkeley: University of California Press, 2004.

———. *Empty Cages: Facing the Challenge of Animal Rights*. New York: Rowman & Littlefield, 2004.

Roberts, Holly H. *Vegetarian Christian Saints*. Calcutta: Anjeli, 2004.

Rollin, B. E. *Animals Rights and Human Morality*. Buffalo: Prometheus, 1992.

Bibliography

———. *The Unheeded Cry: Animal Consciousness, Animal Pain and Science*. Oxford: Oxford University Press, 1990.
The Roman Missal, English Translation. 3rd typical ed. London: Catholic Truth Society, 2011.
Roman Ritual: Book of Blessings. Collegeville, MN: Liturgical Press, 1989.
Rowlands, M. *Animal Rights: Moral Theory and Practice*. 2nd ed. Basingstoke, England: Palgrave Macmillan, 2009.
Ryder, Richard D. *Animal Revolution: Changing Attitudes towards Speciesism*. Oxford: Basil Blackwell, 1989.
———. *Animal Revolution: Changing Attitudes towards Speciesism*. Oxford: Berg, 2000.
———. "Tyrannical Anthropocentrism (2015)." *The Ark*, 90th anniversary ed., 243 (Autumn 2019).
"Saints and Animals." Pan-Orthodox Concern for Animals, n.d. http://panorthodoxconcernforanimals.org/saints-and-animals/.
"Saints Who Loved Animals." Catholic Concern for Animals, n.d. https://catholic-animals.com/saints-who-loved-animals/.
Salt, H. S. *Animals' Rights*. 1892, reprint. Alicia Editions, 2020.
Sargent, T. *Animal Rights and Wrongs: A Biblical Perspective*. London: Hodder and Stoughton, 1996.
Scrutton, R. *Animal Rights and Wrongs*. London: Metro, 2000.
Scully, M. *Dominion: The Power of Man, the Suffering of Animals, and the Call to Mercy*. London: Souvenir, 2011.
Shevelow, K. *For the Love of Animals: The Rise of the Animal Protection Movement*. New York: Henry Holt, 2008.
Singer, Peter. *Animal Liberation Now*. Dublin: Penguin, 2023.
———, ed. *In Defence of Animals*. Oxford: Blackwell, 1985.
Smith, Sally H. "A Review of Andrew Linzey's 'Animal Theology' from a Theological Perspective." *Review and Expositor* 102.1 (2005) 101–9.
Smith, W. J. *A Rat Is a Pig Is a Dog Is a Boy: The Human Cost of the Animal Rights Movement*. New York: Encounter, 2010.
Spalde, A., and P. Strindlund. *Every Creature a Word of God*. Cleveland: Vegetarian Advocates, 2008.
Spencer, C. *The Heretic's Feast: A History of Vegetarianism*. New Hampshire: University Press of New England, 1995.
Spiegel, M. *The Dreaded Comparison: Human and Animal Slavery*. New York: Mirror, 1996.
Stallwood, Kim. *Growl*. New York: Lantern, 2014.
Steck, C. *All God's Animals: A Catholic Theological Framework for Animals Ethics*. Washington, DC: Georgetown University Press, 2019.
Sunstein, C. R., And M. C. Nussbaum, eds. *Animal Rights: Current Debates and New Directions*. New York: Oxford University Press, 2004.
Taylor, A. *Animals and Ethics: An Overview of the Philosophical Debate*. 3rd ed. Ontario: Broadview, 2009.
Tennyson, Alfred. *In Memoriam A. H. H.* South Carolina: CreateSpace Independent, 2017.
Tertullian. *On Prayer*. Self-published, CreateSpace Independent, 2015.
Thigpen, Paul. "Animals in Heaven?" Simply Catholic, n.d. https://www.simplycatholic.com/animals-in-heaven/.

Bibliography

Thomas of Celano. *First Life of St. Francis*. Translated by A. G. Ferrers Howell. London: Methuen, 1926. https://dmdhist.sitehost.iu.edu/francis.htm.

Torrance, Thomas F. *Theology in Reconciliation*. Eugene, OR: Wipf & Stock, 1996.

UK Farm Animal Welfare Council. *Report on the Welfare of Farmed Animals at Slaughter or Killing*. 2003. https://www.gov.uk/government/publications/fawc-report-on-the-welfare-of-farmed-animals-at-slaughter-or-killing,

"UK Government Must Finally Take Action to End CO2 Pig Slaughter." Compassion in World Farming, Sept. 21, 2021. https://www.ciwf.org.uk/media/press-releases-statements/2021/09/uk-government-must-finally-take-action-to-end-co2-pig-slaughter.

Waal, Frans de. *Mama's Last Hug*. London: Granta, 2019.

Waddell, H. *Beasts and Saints*. Edinburgh: Constable & Company, 1960.

Webb, S. H. *On God and Dogs: A Christian Theology of Compassion for Animals*. Oxford: Oxford University Press, 1998.

Wennberg, R. H. *God, Humans, and Animals: An Invitation to Enlarge Our Moral Compass*. Grand Rapids: Eerdmans, 2003.

White, Thomas I. *Discovering Philosophy*. 2nd ed. Saddle River, NJ: Pearson/Prentice Hall, 2007.

Wise, Steven M. *Drawing the Line: Science and the Case for Animal Rights*. Cambridge, MA: Perseus, 2002.

———. *Rattling the Cage*. London: Profile Books, 2000.

York, Tripp, and Andy Alexis-Baker, eds. *A Faith Embracing All Creatures: Addressing Commonly Asked Questions about Christian Care for Animals*. Eugene, OR: Cascade, 2012.

Zuolo, Federico. "The Moral Value of Animal Sentience and Agency." In *Human/Animal Relationships in Transformation*, edited by Augusto Vitale and Simone Pollo, 47–66. Cham, Switzerland: Palgrave Macmillan, 2021.